Farnsworth's Classical English Style

Farnsworth's

CLASSICAl

 DAVID R. GODINE · *Publisher · Boston*

NGLISH STYLE

by WARD FARNSWORTH

Published in 2020 by
David R. Godine, Publisher, Inc.
Boston, Massachusetts
www.godine.com

LIBRARY OF CONGRESS CATALOGING-IN-PUBLICATION DATA

Names: Farnsworth, Ward, 1967– author.
Title: Farnsworth's classical English style / Ward Farnsworth.
Other titles: Classical English style
Description: Boston : David R. Godine, Publisher, 2020. | Includes bibliographical ref-
erences. | Summary: "Farnsworth's Classical English Style is third in a series about prin-
ciples of good writing, derived from an earlier age in the life of the language. While
books on style usually emphasize some general principles, this book spends a lot of
time on details, providing numerous examples of the principles Farnsworth outlines.
Farnsworth asks why good writing sounds that way through many small choices in
words, rhythm, and the construction of sentences and explains how those choices put
force into writing and speech"— Provided by publisher.
Identifiers: LCCN 2019052915 | ISBN 9781567926651 (hardcover)
Subjects: LCSH: English language–Style.
Classification: LCC PE1421 .F37 2020 | DDC 808.02—dc23
LC record available at https://lccn.loc.gov/2019052915

THIRD PRINTING 2021
Printed in the United States of America

CONTENTS

Preface · VII

Introduction · XI

CHAPTER ONE   Simplicity · 1

CHAPTER TWO   The Saxon Finish · 12

CHAPTER THREE   The Latinate Finish and Variations · 24

CHAPTER FOUR   Choice of Words: Special Effects · 32

CHAPTER FIVE   Metonymy · 44

CHAPTER SIX   Hyperbole · 55

CHAPTER SEVEN   The Lengths of Sentences · 64

CHAPTER EIGHT   Sentence Structure · 74

CHAPTER NINE   The Passive Voice · 92

CHAPTER TEN   Anacoluthon and Related Devices · 100

CHAPTER ELEVEN   The Rhetorical Instruction · 112

CHAPTER TWELVE   The Rhetorical Announcement · 121

CHAPTER THIRTEEN   Cadence: Classic Patterns · 126

CHAPTER FOURTEEN   Cadence: Combinations & Contrasts · 138

PREFACE

Abraham Lincoln wrote more beautifully and memorably than anyone in public life does now. So did Winston Churchill; so did Edmund Burke; so did many others, none of whom sound quite alike but all of whom achieved an eloquence that seems foreign to our times. What did they know that we don't? It might seem strange to seek instruction from writers who lived so long ago. It certainly would sound odd to imitate their styles directly. But writers of lasting stature still make the best teachers. They understood principles of style that are powerful and enduring, even if the principles have to be adapted to our era, or to any other, before they become useful. That is the premise of this book, at any rate. It is a set of lessons on style drawn from writers whose words have stood the test of time.

This book is the third in a series. The first, *Classical English Rhetoric*, showed how rhetorical figures – ancient patterns for the arrangement of words – have been used to great effect in English oratory and prose. The second, *Classical English Metaphor*, did the same for figurative comparisons. This one takes a similar approach to more basic questions of style: the selection of words, the arrangement of sentences, the creation of a cadence. It shows how masters of the language have made those choices, and how the choices have put life into their writing and their speech.

That is a short summary of the aim of this project. Below are some other ways to think about it. There are plenty of books already about how to write, many of which are excellent, so it's worth a moment to explain why this one is any different.

A large share of books about prose style are about how to avoid mistakes. They explain why bad writing sounds that way. This book is about stylistic virtue. It asks why good writing sounds that way.

Books on style usually emphasize some general principles. This book also has general principles to offer, but it spends a great deal of attention on details. Some readers will find those details to be too much, but there is no avoiding minutiae if you want to understand why some kinds of writing sound better than others. A style is the result of many small decisions about words, order, tone, cadence, and so on. If you don't have the patience to look hard at little choices like those, that's perfectly reasonable and perhaps a sign of good health. This book is for those who do have the patience because they want to know what has made some heroic writers sound the way they do.

Books on style usually state precepts that have merit but that talented writers violate often. Much of this book is about the violations and reasons to commit them. It often makes sense to be direct, to write active sentences, to avoid Latinate words and long sentences, etc. – but not always. Our topic, in part, is when to make exceptions. A lapse from a supposed rule of style isn't an offense against nature. It's just a choice with consequences, and sometimes you want the consequences.

Typical books about style contain a lot of precepts and a few illustrations of how the precepts work. The ratio in this book is reversed. It depends more on illustrations and supplies them generously. Explaining a precept may take just a few words, but only examples can make it familiar to the *ear*. So we will consider many such examples, and from many sources – from Shakespeare and the King James Bible, from Lincoln and Churchill, from Charles Dickens and Mark Twain, and from other writers and orators who may be a little less famous but who all have lessons to teach.

Most modern books on style use modern examples. The examples in this book are all from writers who died long ago. The book relies on older writers partly because we know that their words have held up well. But it's also because the principles at stake were used with more vigor, prominence, and skill in earlier ages than they are now. A lesson is learned best from those who knew it best themselves. I also think we have more to learn from older writers just because their times are not ours. Their styles offer alternatives to customs that are overly familiar to us. It is true, as a result, that most of the writers featured in this book are white and that most of them are men. That is because the book is focused on an intersection of period and genre that was not equally open to all. I wish the world had been otherwise. Interesting studies might be written about how the same rhetorical ideas have or haven't been used by different people in other times and places. I would welcome those efforts.

Many books assume, for the sake of simplicity, that there is a best way to write for all occasions: modern American house style, it might be called. This book assumes different styles are right for different occasions, and it doesn't try to talk about all of them. It is about how talented writers have achieved eloquence when they needed it. Some of the book is about special effects that are in order only occasionally. Most of us don't need rhetorical force often but might like to do better when it counts. And understanding the springs of eloquence can be useful even when it doesn't count.

Modern books usually just talk about how to make writing clear, simple, and direct – in a word, efficient. This book treats efficiency as important but as not enough if you mean to affect your reader. Rhetorical power doesn't come from just being clear or just being concise or by pushing in any other one direction. It's usually created by some sort of push and pull, or in a word by *contrasts*. The Introduction that follows will explain this idea more fully, and the rest of the book illustrates it in detail.

Most books on style offer advice: write this way, not that way. This book does not offer advice of that kind, let alone formulas; it certainly doesn't say that if you do this or that, you will sound like Lincoln or anyone else. Rhetorical magic is not so easily bottled. But the book does offer some more ideas (to go with the ones from earlier entries in this series) about the elements of style that have made the writings of Lincoln – and Churchill, and Holmes, and others – so compelling.

The approach of this book resembles the indirect tradition from which Lincoln himself learned. He spent long hours reading Shakespeare and the King James Bible – writings from 200 years before he was born. He didn't try to copy them or write as though he were living in the 17th century. He wrote, as everyone must, in a manner acceptable to his own times. Yet his reading still affected him in ways that we hear in his words. Now we can read Lincoln (and Churchill, and others) in something like the way that Lincoln read Shakespeare and the Bible: not to mimic but to listen, learn, and adapt.

This book, in sum, doesn't mean to displace other books about style or put them down. It is just meant to come afterwards. The first thing any writer should learn about, no doubt, is efficiency. But the first thing isn't the last thing, so what comes next? Learning from those who knew other things, too. This book is about some of those other things.

I am grateful to Carl W. Scarbrough for bringing his remarkable talents to the design of the book. For many helpful comments, I thank Kamela Bridges, Alexandra Delp, Ally Findley, Bryan Garner, David Greenwald, Harris Kerr, Andrew Kull, Richard Lanham, David Mamet, Daniel Norland, Nadia Oussayef, Brian Pérez-Daple, Geoffrey Pullum, Christopher Ricks, Christopher Roberts, Wayne Schiess, and Emily Tucker. They are not responsible for mistakes or misjudgments that might remain.

INTRODUCTION

A recurring theme appears at various points in this book, so I wish to summarize it here at the outset. It is that rhetorical power can be created by various sorts of oppositions – by the relationship, usually one of friction or contrast, between two things. The two things might be plain and fancy words, long and short sentences, hard and soft syllables, high or rich substance and low or simple style (or vice versa), the concrete and the abstract, the passive and the active, the dignified and the coarse, detachment from the audience and engagement with it. Other polarities can produce rhetorical current, too, but those are the ones that will mostly occupy us here.

Often the opposition in the foreground of a piece of writing is just between the reader's expectations and what the writer delivers – but the reader's expectations are typically produced by what the writer has already done. If a sentence seems striking for its brevity, for example, that is probably because the writer set it up with sentences that were longer. The writer creates expectations for the listener's ear, then does something a little different. The surprise or contrast may be harmonious or startling, and (if well executed) subtle and indeed subliminal. But such movement creates energy. The energy can be used to affect an audience in various ways: to move them, to amuse them, to hold their attention, to drive a point home.

Movement between poles might be described as rhythm, so long as we remember that rhythm, while sometimes literal (the pulse of the syllables in a sentence), can also be conceptual (as with alternations in tone). I do not mean to suggest that power can be achieved *only* with contrasts and rhythms, but they are immense rhetorical resources; they put fizz into writing. This book sets out in part to demonstrate that claim, and to show practically how some different sorts of contrasts can be created and with what results. If you end up persuaded of the general principle, other applications will be interesting to find elsewhere. When you hear eloquence, you can ask whether and where an opposition of one kind or another has helped to produce its sound.

The theory just stated seems obvious in many arts. But it is contrary to the theory, stated or implied, of most modern books about how to write well. Their advice usually treats just one aim as really important: efficiency. The best writing is the clearest and most concise, period. That approach follows from a simple vision of the writer's goal. The purpose of a piece of writing is to transmit meaning to the reader; so the writer's job is to make the meaning easy to understand, and to keep demands on the reader – the "cognitive load" – to a minimum. You do that by using simple words, writing short sentences, and being direct. Needless words, needless length, or needless anything are inefficiencies, and the writer's job is to eliminate them. The books will sometimes say that lengths of sentences should be varied to avoid monotony, but otherwise contrast is not treated as mattering much.

I have nothing to say against efficiency. I try for it like anyone else. Usually being clear and concise is the best thing a writer can do, and sometimes it's the only thing a writer should worry about. But though efficiency is the most important value in most kinds of writing, it isn't the *only* value. Lincoln's writing is clear, but most writing that is clear sounds nothing like Lincoln's and has none of its beauty or strength. Writing can be clear and energetic, clear and dramatic, clear and full of fire. It can also be clear without any of those qualities. Our culture of advice doesn't explain what made the words of Lincoln or any other master so potent, and usually doesn't try; it seeks ease for the reader but provides no tools for thinking about the other ways in which words can succeed. This book doesn't solve the mystery of Lincoln, either – no book quite can – but it does mean to shed light on a significant aspect of his style: his instinct for oppositions and contrasts.

And we will see that instinct in many other writers, too, though they all have their own styles; nobody would confuse a paragraph from Lincoln with a paragraph from Churchill, though the two of them use many of the same rhetorical ideas. Nor would anyone confuse either of them with Oliver Wendell Holmes, Jr., who is justly regarded as the best writer in the history of American law. But Holmes has his reputation for some of the same reasons that Lincoln and Churchill have theirs. He used longer words *and* shorter words more than most other writers (and all other judges). His sentences were like his words: his long ones were longer than the long sentences that judges write today, and his short sentences were shorter. Holmes had an artful feel for contrasts, in other words, and his writings are infused with them. He sounds like nobody but himself, but he made use of the same general principles that have lent strength to the words of many others.

Lincoln is a crucial figure for this book in another way not yet mentioned. I claim that efficiency isn't enough to make writing great. This might be mistaken for a claim that writing needs to sound fancy to be forceful. Or it might sound like an argument against a so-called Attic or plain style and in favor of a style that is ornamental and (to borrow another ancient term) Asiatic. But that isn't what I mean. The difference that we will see isn't between plain and fancy or Attic and Asiatic. It's between monotony and variation; it's the difference between just throwing fastballs and knowing how to change speeds. Lincoln is important to these claims because he helps prove them. He is famous for having a plain and direct style. Nobody thinks of his speech or writing as purple. Yet we will see that he was a master of the principles that are the subject of this book. He used contrast and movement to lasting effect, and without the least bit of pomposity or pretension.

The ideas just sketched will recur often in this book. It's possible (though not necessary) to view all the chapters to come as applications of them. Each chapter takes up a certain kind of alternation and shows how able writers have put it to use. The early chapters involve alternation between plain and fancy words, the concrete and the abstract, the literal and the exaggerated. The middle chapters are about variety at the level of the sentence: active and passive, right- and left-branching, or direct and indirect approaches to the audience. The last chapters are about the rhythm of prose in a more literal sense – that is, the cadences created by different kinds of syllables.

The chapters will isolate examples of alternation to make them more visible. In practice, of course, alternation tends to be neither isolated nor visible. The writer uses it by feel and the reader experiences it by feel. The consequences don't often call attention to themselves, though we will see dramatic examples where they do. Major and obvious swings between high and low tend to be most apparent in oratory, invective, and other occasions of high rhetorical intensity. So be it; I would appreciate better oratory and invective. But in any event, dramatic examples show how principles work, and the principles can then be adapted to less dramatic settings. You can learn from the Gettysburg Address even if you aren't writing a Gettysburg Address.

I wish to comment, finally, on the current relevance of the principles discussed in this book, and of older examples to illustrate them.

When the *Yale Book of Quotations* was published in 2007, the *New York Times Book Review* was puzzled by the absence of entries in the book from writers born since 1950. The editor asked, "What happened to the literary fiction (and nonfiction) of the last 25 years?" He continued: "If one could compile an anthology of the best things that have been written in the last couple of decades, what would it look like? And: Is it worth trying to compile it?" He invited readers to submit their favorites, and said they would be published on the back page of a future issue.

I looked forward to that issue because I couldn't imagine it. Current customs about rhetoric don't encourage the creation of great and memorable sentences that lend themselves to the kind of display the *Times* proposed. Usually the apex of modern achievement is a sentence that sets new standards for informality. So I was sorry but not surprised when the editor conceded defeat a month later. He reported that the *Times* had received submissions, but not enough that were a fit to the stated criteria. "Many of the quotes weren't from writers at all, or were from quite old (or quite dead) ones. So the plan to print a page of them is out the window," he said. They did receive a few that he felt were deserving of honorable mention: "From space, astronauts can see people making love as a tiny speck of light." "I did not pan out." "I am the zoom." I did not feel that these entries called the editor's overall judgment into question.

This episode helps to show why writers from earlier periods make better teachers of many principles of eloquence. But the limiting customs that made the *Times* exercise so difficult admittedly mean, too, that some of the contrasts we will talk about aren't as available to the writer anymore. Holmes produced remarkable results by putting long sentences next to short ones. Today long sentences are disfavored, though, and many readers lose patience with them; attention spans and reading habits have been conditioned to expect everything shorter. The same goes for choosing words. We will see what can be accomplished by putting Latinate and Saxon words near each other. But the rhetorical sparks created by Holmes or Burke with those methods can be harder to produce now because readers have less patience for Latinate words in the first place. They give up on Burke because they think he sounds flowery, so the writer who wants to use Burke's rhetorical ideas is obliged to tone them down.

In effect some instruments have been removed from the orchestra that the writer conducts. Sentences can't be as long, nor can words. Nor can you get away with a kind of formality that once had delicious rhetorical use. The elimination of these resources is a rhetorical misfortune. A larger loss is the general lack of appreciation for what contrasts can do, and its replacement by admiration for the bland. Many who care about writing have been raised to value clarity and don't know how to notice anything else. This might seem unimportant; if people can no longer either produce or hear rhetorical power, what difference does it make? But I think they do hear it and are moved by it when it is present. They just aren't conscious of it and have no tools for explaining its presence or absence.

The problem arises in the criticism of writing as well as in the creation of it. Those who wring their hands about the decline of the language sometimes worry too much about the wrong things. They observe with horror that people confuse *uninterested* with *disinterested*, or don't know when to say *fewer* and when to say *less*, or fumble in their use of the apostrophe or other punctuation marks. I share a due sense of irritation about points like those. But the more meaningful decline of the language doesn't involve the presence of mistakes. It involves absences that are easier to overlook: the abandonment of half the orchestra, the erosion of rhetorical ability, the dwindling of attention spans, the scarcity of speech that inspires and rouses and strikes deep. A politician rises in a debate and speaks with utter vacuity and with the rhetorical sophistication of an adolescent. The modern guardian of English usage tends to look on without comment or alarm because the statesman was free from error. He was merely terrible.

Regardless, one consequence of this state of affairs should be stated outright so that nobody starts this book with the wrong idea. Some of the ideas to come are useful in obvious ways now. Some aren't. But I think the ones not as directly useful are still part of a thoughtful writer's knowledge. By way of comparison, this might resemble a book about how certain types of buildings or movies were made in the past. Architects or film directors with respect for their craft will find those principles valuable to understand, even if the demands of clients and audiences now require their use to be sparing or indirect. It's worth knowing how great things have been done in the past, whether or not we can do all of them now.

And meanwhile rhetoric matters today more than ever, though sometimes in ways that aren't as apparent as they once were. It has been a long time since a large share of the public had patience for the kinds of speeches that Lincoln or Churchill gave. At present it's not clear if the public has patience for an utterance that takes more than a minute or two to read or hear. But if that's true, one must make the most of one's minute. In a world where everyone has a printing press, understanding words and their consequences becomes more important, not less.

It's also natural to ask what relevance these ideas about rhetoric could have in an era when Donald Trump was elected President of the United States. Lincoln is one of this book's heroes, and from a rhetorical standpoint Trump might be considered the anti-Lincoln. But Trump confirms the importance of our subject. A large part of his appeal was rhetorical. He, too, was a user of polarities, and in a way he illustrates well the central claim of this book. His way of talking was unlike that of his adversaries. Here was a rich and famous presidential candidate making schoolyard taunts of his rivals, joking about the size of his private parts, and saying whatever shocking thing came to his mind. Put dignified language into his mouth and he amounts to nothing; put his undignified language into the mouth of someone with ordinary status, and he too would amount to nothing. But such a casual lack of dignity in a tycoon, television star, and presidential candidate – this was something! A more vivid collision of high and low would be hard to devise, and many people have found it compelling or amusing enough to make all objections seem trivial.

This book isn't quite about *that* sort of rhetorical polarity – not principally, anyway. It's about other polarities that have been effective in the hands of talented writers and talkers. The methods of earlier eras may not be working as well as the methods of Trump under current conditions (though let us not jump to conclusions; Trump was not challenged by a Lincoln). Even if so, however, the comings and goings of such methods, and their appeal, tend to run in cycles. The first principles behind various forms of rhetorical power are always worthy of study – or, failing that, fun to know about – no matter what shape they are taking at the moment.

Chapter One

SIMPLICITY

There are two ways to say almost anything in English: with little words or big ones. More precisely, you can say most things with older, shorter words that have Germanic (or "Saxon") roots, or with longer words that came into the language more recently – perhaps six or seven hundred years ago – from French, and before that from Latin. Our first topic is the difference between those types of words and how to choose between them.

1. *Two languages in one*. English is a language built mostly out of two others. Much of it was founded on the language of invaders who came to Britain around 450 A.D. from Anglia and Saxony, in what is now northern Germany. We don't know much about the language spoken in Britain before then (Common Brittonic); in any event, the languages the invaders brought with them turned into the tongue we now call Old English, or Anglo-Saxon – the language of *Beowulf*. Many people now associate the expression "Anglo-Saxon" with England. If you want to understand how the English language works, it helps to grasp that those terms refer originally to places in Germany.

About 600 years later the French invaded Britain, and they, too, brought their language with them. Unlike the Germanic languages already there, the French of the new round of invaders was derived from Latin. The new French competed with Old English, and the eventual outcome was a language – modern English – built out of both.

This process of making a new language out of two old ones took several hundred years. Often words with similar meanings from the two languages were both turned into English words, such as *make* (Saxon) and *create* (from French), or *need* (Saxon) and *require* (from French). There have been many contributions to the language from elsewhere, too, so this account is oversimplified for the sake of brevity. The point is just that most common things still can be said using Saxon words or Latinate words. And those terms themselves are approximations. We will use "Saxon" as shorthand for words of roughly Germanic origin (some might actually have their etymologies in old Norse, etc.). By "Latinate" words we mean any derived from Latin (though in a few cases their roots might be Greek).

2. *General differences.* So English is a mongrel language, and this creates choices for its users. They can pick their words from two lines of descent. The two kinds of words are usually easy enough to tell apart. In a moment we will talk about why; first, though, see for yourself. Here are some examples of Saxon and Latinate verbs, nouns, and adjectives with similar meanings. Observe how the words in the Saxon column are generally different from the words in the Latinate column.

Saxon	Latinate	Saxon	Latinate
See	Perceive	Luck	Fortune
Ask	Inquire	Share	Proportion
Come	Arrive	Shot	Injection
Let	Permit	Break	Respite
Eat	Ingest	Small	Diminutive
Break	Damage	High	Elevated
Mark	Designate	Fair	Equitable
Grow	Cultivate	Good	Favorable
House	Residence	Next	Subsequent
Tool	Implement	Last	Final
Kin	Relatives	Right	Correct
Talk	Conversation	Tight	Constricting

We could go on with these lists. It's a fine parlor game to name a Latinate equivalent for every Saxon word you can think of. You can do it even if you don't know any French or German. Saxon words are shorter, and in their simplest forms they usually consist of just one syllable. Latinate words usually have a root of two or three syllables, and then can be lengthened further and turned into other parts of speech.

The simplest guide, useful often but not always, is this: if a word ends with *-tion*, or if it could be made into a similar word that does, then it almost always is derived from Latin. Same if it easily takes other suffixes that turn it into a longish word. Thus the Latinate word *acquire* can become *acquisition* or *acquisitive*; but the equivalent Germanic word *get* doesn't take new endings in this way. It can change tenses or forms (into *got* or *getting*) but it can't be turned into a four-syllable noun or adjective the way *acquire* can.

Now consider some more specific differences between the two kinds of words.

3. *Sound.* Saxon words tend to sound different from Latinate words in ways distantly related to the sounds of the modern German and French languages. Many Saxon words have hard sounds like *ck* or the hard *g*. Latinate words are usually softer and more mellifluous.

4. *Tone: high vs. low; formal vs. informal.* When French arrived in England it was the language of the conqueror and the new nobility. A thousand years later, words from French still connote a certain fanciness and distance from the gritty, and Saxon words still seem plainer, less formal, and closer to the earth. If you want to talk clinically about something distasteful, you use the Latinate word for it – the one derived from old French: *terminate* or *execute* (Latinate) instead of *kill* (Saxon).

And as you would expect, forbidden words – "swear words" – tend to be Saxon. The most famous taboo word in the language is a good example, being short (a "four-letter" word) and ending with the familiar hard sound; its precise etymology is unknown but probably

Germanic. The Latinate equivalent – *copulate* – is longer, sounds softer, takes suffixes, seems more distant from the act, and can be said in polite company. Anyone can think of other examples that work the same way. These distinctions used to be understood more widely, and could be made a subject for public comment more easily than they are today.

Cobden, speech in the House
of Commons (1862)

Now comes this flagrant specimen of the noble Lord's inexactness. I purposely use that long and rather French word because I wish to be Parliamentary in what I say.

Williams, speech in the Senate
(1913)

The removal of the duty will serve one good purpose, and that will be to undeceive – or, if I may frame a strong Saxon word, to unfool – the farmers who have been deceived and fooled by political oratory and literature for so many years to believe that increasing prices are due to the tariff.

Exchange in the Senate (1906)

MR. TILLMAN. The Senator always quibbles, however, if I may use that word, in some of his answers. I do not say that offensively. MR. SPOONER. The Senator has used the word "quibbles." He did not intend it to be offensive – MR. TILLMAN. No, indeed. MR. SPOONER. But it is. MR. TILLMAN. I will take it back, and I will ask the Senator to correct me if I am wrong. . . I do not want to use the word "dodge" – another Saxon word – and therefore I am at a loss as to what to say, unless I were to get a thesaurus or use some word that would be Latinized, perhaps.

But words from French aren't just euphemisms for things said more directly with words from old English. Latinate words are often the more natural choice and occasionally the only choice for talking about a subject, especially something intellectual in character. As the conceptual life of English speakers became more sophisticated, they

needed new words to talk about what they were thinking. They usually made them out of French or more
directly from Latin or Greek. That is part of why people
who teach at universities find it hard to prefer Saxon
words when they have their conversations. Most of them
would probably write better if they *did* use more Saxon
words, but there are lots of tempting Latinate words that
seem designed for academic purposes, because they were.
They allow a kind of precision (or facilitate a kind of
jargon) that Saxon words cannot match.

5. *Visual vs. conceptual; felt vs. thought.* Saxon words tend
to be easier to picture than the Latinate kind, most of
which need a minor moment of translation before they
appear in the mind's eye. Compare *light* (Saxon) and *illu-
mination* (Latinate), *bodily* (Saxon) and *corporeal* (Latinate), *burn* (Saxon) and *incinerate* (Latinate). The
difference between visual and conceptual is related to
the ways that these kinds of words can speak to the different capacities of an audience. Latinate words tend to
create distance from what they describe. They invite
thought but not feeling. Saxon words are more visceral.
They take a shorter path to the heart.

These features of Saxon and Latinate words are just
tendencies. Some Latinate words, such as *brave* or *fact* or
catch or *count*, sound Saxon. So it's a mistake to go hunt-
ing for a Saxon word. It isn't always easy to tell which
words are which; if you want a word that has Saxon qualities, you are better off just picking one that is simple and
concrete rather than fussing over its etymology – for no
one cares about its etymology.

The point is general. We aren't principally interested
in where words came from. We care about what they
mean, what they sound like, and how they feel. We could
just talk directly about those qualities and ignore all else.
But the origins of words are still helpful and interesting
to grasp because they help explain why words have the

sound they do. Understanding the terms is also conve-
nient, because referring to Saxon or Latinate words is an
easy way to refer to all those qualities mentioned a
moment ago, which otherwise would be tedious to
recount and make many words hard to classify. So the
chapters to come will often make use of those labels. But
if this is all too much, or too confusing – or if you just
want a simpler way to think about the point when writing – go back to where we started: you can say almost
anything in English with two families of words, the
fancy or the simple.

6. *Prefer Saxon words.* Having made this summary of the
kinds of words that the writer of English can use, turn to
the practical question of how to choose between them.
Which should it be – big words or little, Latinate words
or Saxon? Students of style who discuss the point are
unanimous in their answer: prefer small words and
Saxon words, which are usually the same. As the Fowler
brothers put it in 1906:

Prefer the familiar word to the far-fetched.

Prefer the concrete word to the abstract.

Prefer the single word to the circumlocution.

Prefer the short word to the long.

Prefer the Saxon word to the Romance.

(By "Romance" they basically meant Latinate; Latin was
the language of Rome, so Romance languages are those
such as French that are descended from Latin.) Or
Strunk and White: "Anglo-Saxon is a livelier tongue than
Latin, so use Anglo-Saxon words." Or Churchill: "The
shorter words of a language are usually the more ancient.
Their meaning is more ingrained in the national character and they appeal with greater force to simple under-
standings than words recently introduced from the Latin

and the Greek." Churchill again: "Broadly speaking, short
words are best, and the old words, when short, are best of
all." Orwell expressed the idea this way:

> Bad writers, and especially scientific, political and
> sociological writers, are nearly always haunted by
> the notion that Latin or Greek words are grander
> than Saxon ones, and unnecessary words like *expe-
> dite, ameliorate, predict, extraneous, deracinated,
> clandestine, sub-aqueous* and hundreds of others
> constantly gain ground from their Anglo-Saxon
> opposite numbers.

Orwell, *Politics and the English
Language* (1946)

Samuel Johnson is a study in the contrast between the
styles produced by these different sorts of words. Boswell's *Life of Johnson* endlessly records Johnson's speech,
which tends to be funny, memorable, and often highly
Saxon. (We will see examples soon.) When Johnson
wrote, however, he used a high density of Latinate words,
as a result of which his writing style – "Johnsonese" –
now seems repulsive to most people in anything other
than small doses:

> ... so much was every one solicitous for my regard,
> that I could seldom escape to solitude, or steal a
> moment from the emulation of complaisance,
> and the vigilance of officiousness.

The Rambler no. 142 (1751)

In response to this sort of writing, Macaulay said of
Johnson:

> All his books are written in a learned language, in
> a language which nobody hears from his mother
> or his nurse, in a language in which nobody ever
> quarrels, or drives bargains, or makes love, in a
> language in which nobody ever thinks.... he felt a
> vicious partiality for terms which, long after our
> own speech had been fixed, were borrowed from
> the Greek and Latin, and which, therefore, even

Macaulay, *Samuel Johnson*
(1831)

when lawfully naturalized, must be considered as born aliens, not entitled to rank with the king's English.

Sticking with Saxon words is usually sound advice, especially if it helps beat back the idea that impressive prose is made out of impressive words. For most people most of the time, attractive English isn't the art of choosing beautiful words. It is the art of arranging humble words beautifully.

7. *The King James Bible.* The power of simple words is put on famous exhibit in the King James Bible. It contains many well-known verses that consist entirely of Saxon words, and sometimes just words of one syllable.

Gen. 1:3

And God said, Let there be light: and there was light.

Matt. 7:7

Ask, and it shall be given you; seek, and ye shall find; knock, and it shall be opened unto you.

John 8:32

And ye shall know the truth, and the truth shall make you free.

John 15:13

Greater love hath no man than this, that a man lay down his life for his friends.

Every word of those passages is Saxon. The gravity of their meaning matches the simplicity of their wording. Perhaps more precisely, the sense of weight is increased by the *contrast* between the size of the meanings and the size of the words. A big thing has been pressed into a small container. The result is a type of tension. It gets released in the mind of the reader.

8. *Shakespeare.* Examples of heavily Saxon passages from Shakespeare are easy to think of as well. He, too, would use small words to compress large meanings, but he also had aims more complex. He often sought in various ways to align the sound of his language with the substance of it.

In sooth I know not why I am so sad.   *The Merchant of Venice*, 1, 1

The lowly words help along the somber feeling. The complexity in the speaker also is set off against the simplicity of the language.

> If it were done when 'tis done, then 'twere well   *Macbeth*, 1, 7
> It were done quickly.

The speaker is considering murder. (If it would put an end to his troubles, best to do it right away.) The enormity of the idea is heightened by the contrast with the little and indirect words used to talk about it.

> Upon what meat doth this our Cæsar feed,   *Julius Cæsar*, 1, 2
> That he is grown so great? Age, thou art shamed!

Saxon words are most suitable for the purpose of the speaker: exposing what is overinflated. He spits forth his indignation in words of one syllable. For breaking up and tearing down, Saxon words make a strong chisel. They have the ring of plain truth.

It might seem strange to hold these examples up as illustrating anything in particular. No one would read them and be struck by their Saxon character. But notice the effects that such words can support without calling attention to themselves.

9. *Lincoln.* Abraham Lincoln, who spent a lot of time reading Shakespeare and the King James Bible, was likewise famous for his simple words and the plain sound that came from them.

> If we could first know where we are, and whither   Lincoln, "House Divided"
> we are tending, we could then better judge what   speech at Springfield (1858)
> to do, and how to do it.

> Let us have faith that right makes might, and in   Lincoln, speech at Cooper
> that faith, let us, to the end, dare to do our duty as   Union (1860)
> we understand it.

Lincoln, Gettysburg Address
(1863)

The world will little note, nor long remember what we say here, but it can never forget what they did here.

Most of these words are Saxon. (A few are Latinate in origin – "tending" and "judge" and "duty," for example – but they are short and humble anyway.) They make a claim sound credible. Simple words seem incapable of duplicity; unadorned language suggests unadorned truth. In each case there is the usual drama, too, in the contrast between the magnitude of the substance and the size of the words.

10. *Churchill.* Winston Churchill, too, knew well how to put simple Saxon words into an order that made them compelling. He often arranged them in time-honored ways that increase their impact, such as the repetition of structure and of words in these examples.

Churchill, London radio
broadcast (1940)

We are fighting *by* ourselves alone; but we are not fighting *for* ourselves alone.

Churchill, London radio
broadcast (1940)

We seek to beat the life and soul out of Hitler and Hitlerism. That alone, that all the time, that to the end.

Churchill, London radio
broadcast (1940)

"What is it that Britain and France are fighting for?" To this I answer: "If we left off fighting you would soon find out."

We see that homely words need not make for homely sentences. The art is moved to the choice and arrangement of them. Readers who consider eloquent speech with this principle in mind will find examples of it often enough. "These are the times that try men's souls" – all Saxon words (except maybe *try*), and see how their beauty is spoiled by changing the order in various ways.

In those cases from Churchill, we also see again contrast – by now familiar – between the modesty of the words and the height of the substance. The discrepancy is filled in by feeling that the reader or listener supplies.

We shall go on to the end, we shall fight in France, we shall fight on the seas and oceans, we shall fight with growing confidence and growing strength in the air, we shall defend our Island, whatever the cost may be, we shall fight on the beaches, we shall fight on the landing grounds, we shall fight in the fields and in the streets, we shall fight in the hills; we shall never surrender.

Churchill, speech in the
House of Commons (1940)

In that passage are six Latinate words, 69 Saxon. Saving the most prominent Latinate word for the end is an idea we will consider more closely in a later chapter.

The point: short and simple words are the good writer's staple. Part of the reason is the usual one found in many books about style: changing Latinate words into Saxon equivalents will tend to make any piece of writing more powerful, clear, and direct. But this chapter has also sought to show that Saxon words have further advantages that might be called rhetorical. They aid credibility. Their sound can reinforce the substance of a claim. And using small words to express large ideas can produce energy. The ideas seem to strain the words at their seams – a case of contrast not between different types of words but between substance and diction. Sticking to Saxon words also helps to focus rhetorical effort on their order, a matter in need of more attention than it often gets. So if you want a rule to live by as a writer, let it be a preference for Saxon words.

But the best writers don't live by one rule.

Chapter Two

THE SAXON FINISH

As we have seen, most advisers on style recommend using the simplest words possible – to prefer Saxon over Latinate. This advice would be sound if you wanted a single rule of thumb. But it doesn't quite explain the choice of words in the strongest writing, especially the kind that achieves effects beyond the mere transmission of meaning. The best writers – or anyway writers of a certain distinguished kind – mix Saxon and Latinate words artfully.

The mixing can have various consequences. The use of longer, nicer words can set off shorter and plainer ones; each gives relief from the other and can cause the other to stand out. Short words also can be read faster than long ones, and skilled writers, like musicians, don't always play at the same speed. Longer words that slow the reader can create an appetite for acceleration, and so lend strength to the short words that come next. And good writing has variety in the *sounds* that it makes, in whether it is more or less refined, in whether it is abstract or concrete, and in whether it appeals to the heart or mind. All those variations create rhetorical energy that can be put to various uses, as by enabling a writing or a speech to convince, inspire, or scathe.

These first chapters look at some classic ways that writers have mixed plain and fancy words. I do not mean to suggest that any pattern is better than any other. They are just ways to create different results. The first, and our subject here, is the use of Saxon words to end sentences that begin with a Latinate flavor (or the use of whole Saxon sentences to follow Latinate ones). Starting with Latinate words creates a sense of height and abstraction. Ending with plain language brings the sentence onto

land. The simplicity of the finish can also lend it a conclusive ring. And the longer words give the shorter ones
a power, by force of contrast, that the shorter ones would
not have had alone.

1. *The King James Bible.* We saw that the King James version of the Bible is known for its use of simple words to
say large things. But the translators of the KJV also used
other principles to create some of their most beautiful
sentences. Here are three Biblical examples of using Saxon
words to finish off a sentence that starts the other way:

> Every kingdom divided against itself is brought to
> desolation; and every city or house divided against
> itself shall not stand.

Matt. 13:25

> But he was wounded for our transgressions, he
> was bruised for our iniquities: the chastisement of
> our peace was upon him; and with his stripes we
> are healed.

Isa. 53:5

> Thou preparest a table before me in the presence
> of mine enemies: thou anointest my head with
> oil; my cup runneth over.

Psalm 23:5

This, too, is the sound of the King James Bible and an
influential pattern in English prose. In each case a Latinate feel is established early in the sentence or toward its
middle (with words such as *divided, desolation, transgres-
sions, iniquities, presence, anoint*). Then the sentence ends
with plain, Saxon words that are made more striking by
comparison. The Saxon finish also provides a kind of
punctuation in sound. The plain words pull the loftier
sentiments to the ground and create closure.

In those first examples the Latinate diction was
strewn throughout the first three-quarters of the sentence. But sometimes a Latinate word does its work just
at the start, with the rest of the sentence rolling forward
in Saxon fashion.

Matt. 6:34

Sufficient unto the day is the evil thereof.

Matt. 22:21

Render therefore unto Cæsar the things which are Cæsar's; and unto God the things that are God's.

Sufficient is a Latinate word. The movement from there to the Saxon ones that follow, and the cadence started by its three syllables, are essential to the music of the first sentence. The same can be said for *render* (and perhaps also *Cæsar*) in the second one. The simple language at the end is set up by the different language at the start.

2. *Shakespeare*. Shakespeare's uses of the Saxon finish display some more particular patterns that we will see repeated elsewhere. First is the use of Saxon language to restate, in simpler words, what was just said in longer ones.

Macbeth, 2, 2

Will all great Neptune's ocean wash this blood
Clean from my hand? No, this my hand will rather
The multitudinous seas incarnadine,
Making the green one red.

As we've seen, Shakespeare also liked to choose words that would cause the diction to follow the substance, as here:

Julius Cæsar, 4, 2

When love begins to sicken and decay,
It useth an enforced ceremony.
There are no tricks in plain and simple faith.

The fancy words are used to describe a false possibility, and simple words are used to express a true one.

Julius Cæsar, 3, 2

Ambition should be made of sterner stuff.

The way that a phrase such as "sterner stuff" hits the ear depends on how it has been set up by the rest of the sentence. The pattern of this last line is a bit like *Sufficient unto the day is the evil thereof*: a Latinate start (*ambition*) that then unfolds in simple fashion. The contrast between the words mirrors the claim itself.

3. *Lincoln.* Lincoln liked to end with simple Saxon words, especially after using the Latinate variety earlier. This combination helped produce a sound that is one of signatures of his style.

> I believe this government cannot endure permanently half *slave* and half *free*.

Lincoln, speech at Republican State Convention in Springfield (1858)

The sentence starts out Latinate; most of the words are polysyllabic. It ends with five words of one syllable. "Slave" is Latinate, but has properties we normally associate with Saxon words. It is visual, simple, and short. The last five words are made to stand out by the words that set them up. From a moment later in the same speech:

> Either the *opponents* of slavery will arrest the further spread of it, and place it where the public mind shall rest in the belief that it is in the course of ultimate extinction; or its *advocates* will push it forward till it shall become alike lawful in all the States, *old* as well as *new*, *North* as well as *South*.

Lincoln, speech at Republican State Convention in Springfield (1858)

The first half of the sentence has lots of Latinate words: *opponents, slavery, arrest, course, ultimate, extinction, advocates.* Then it ends with 14 words of one syllable in a row, all of them Saxon except "States" (which might as well be). He expresses the hope in large, uplifting words, and the threat in words that are short and simple.

> But the proclamation, as law, either is valid or is not valid. If it is not valid it needs no retraction. If it is valid it cannot be retracted, any more than the dead can be brought to life.

Lincoln, letter to James Conkling (1863)

The key words in the first three-quarters of the sentence are Latinate: *proclamation, valid,* and *retraction,* with the latter two repeated in various ways. The last ten words are all Saxon monosyllables. The legalistic talk about validity and retraction is reduced to something that anyone can understand.

Lincoln, speech at Baltimore (1864)

> We all declare for liberty; but in using the same *word* we do not all mean the same *thing*.

The first half of the sentence is Latinate (*declare, liberty, using*). Then it ends with 11 Saxon monosyllables. What we all claim to do is stated in high language. The hard truth is stated plainly.

Lincoln, Thanksgiving Proclamation (1863)

> We have been the recipients of the choicest bounties of Heaven. We have been preserved, these many years, in peace and prosperity. We have grown in numbers, wealth and power, as no other nation has ever grown. But we have forgotten God.

The passage starts out Latinate and ends Saxon. The progress of the diction follows the progress of the thought, from the luxuries that have been enjoyed to the simple thing that has been neglected. A last example:

Lincoln, Second Inaugural Address (1865)

> Both parties deprecated war, but one of them would *make* war rather than let the nation survive, and the other would *accept* war rather than let it perish, and the war came.

A fine instance of a simple finish used for the sake of contrast. The opinions and purposes of the parties are expressed in Latinate words (*deprecate, nation, survive, accept, perish*). The fact of what happened next is stated in solemn words of one syllable. Large words for complex intentions, plain words for plain truths.

The sound of Lincoln's prose is made of many elements. This is just one of them, but it is important. Lincoln is well-known for his love of simple language, but he was also at home with Latinate words and mixed the two types to strong effect. He especially liked to circle with larger words early in a sentence and then finish it simply. The pattern allowed him to offer intellectual or idealistic substance and then tie it to a stake in the dirt.

4. *Churchill.* Churchill also was a master of movement from one kind of word to another.

> Never in the field of human conflict was so much owed by so many to so few.

Churchill, speech in the House of Commons (1940)

"Human conflict" is Latinate; every word after it is Saxon. More simply put, the earlier part of the sentence has more complicated words than the later part. The first half sets up the ear for the second, which gains strength by contrast.

> This is only the first sip, the first foretaste of a bitter cup which will be proffered to us year by year unless by a supreme recovery of moral health and martial vigor, we arise again and take our stand for freedom as in the olden time.

Churchill, speech in the House of Commons (1938)

In "supreme recovery of moral health and martial vigor," five out of the six major words (nouns and adjectives) are Latinate. In "we arise again and take our stand for freedom as in the olden time," he ends with 14 Saxon words in a row. The Latin phrase is abstract and speaks to the mind and ideals of the audience. The remainder of the sentence, which ended the speech, uses old and simple words that create feeling.

Churchill sometimes used the qualities of Saxon words to offset the mood created by longer and more ambitious ones. The fancier words make their point up in the air; the simple words at the end plant the speaker's feet, usually in a way that limits or counters whatever was said more grandly.

> This truth is incontrovertible. Panic may resent it, ignorance may deride it, malice may distort it, but there it is.

Churchill, speech in the House of Commons (1916)

> President Roosevelt is the object of a good many jibes and taunts from the German Fuhrer. The President's high purpose and great station will

Churchill, speech to the United States (1939)

enable him to rise superior to these. The American democracy is likewise subjected to ridicule. They will get over that.

Churchill, London radio broadcast (1940)

As you know, I have always – after some long and hard experience – spoken with the utmost restraint and caution about the war at sea, and I am quite sure that there are many losses and misfortunes which lie ahead of us there; but in all humility and self-questioning I feel able to declare that at the Admiralty, as, I have no doubt, at the French Ministry of Marine, things are not going so badly after all.

After a Latinate start, the casual Saxon finish is refreshing. It suggests that the speaker is dealing in realities. It creates a sense of familiarity, too, and so closes the distance between speaker and audience for a moment. Churchill would also move from fancy to simple words to underscore a contrast between high and low truths.

Churchill, remark to Harold Macmillan (1943)

You may take the most gallant sailor, the most intrepid airman, or the most audacious soldier, put them at a table together – what do you get? The sum of their fears.

"Sum" is Latinate, so we can just consider that passage a case of big words followed by little ones.

Churchill, speech in the House of Commons (1938)

They will never understand how it was that a victorious nation, with everything in hand, suffered themselves to be brought low, and to cast away all that they had gained by measureless sacrifice and absolute victory – gone with the wind!

Of course *measureless sacrifice* and *absolute victory* are Latinate words. *Gone with the wind* is all Saxon. The abrupt movement from one to the other underscores the substance: the sudden and shocking loss of precious things.

5. *Holmes*. Oliver Wendell Holmes, Jr., as noted in the introduction, is widely considered the best writer that American law has had. He is sometimes said to have used a plain style. That reputation contains some truth; it comes from his frankness, dislike of pretense, and distaste for rhetorical ornament, all of which are the linguistic side of his acidic view of the world. But he also had the gifted writer's instinct for variety.

> If there is any principle of the Constitution that more imperatively calls for attachment than any other it is the principle of free thought – not free thought for those who agree with us but freedom for the thought that we hate.

Holmes, *United States v. Schwimmer* (dissenting opinion) (1929)

The part of the sentence before the dash is dominated by Latinate words – *popular, prejudice, principle, Constitution, imperatively, attachment, principle* (again). The part after the dash, and especially the finish, takes a turn toward the simple: 19 words, all but one of which are Saxon. This was a characteristic pattern for Holmes. After working with large words and concepts for a while, he would ground a claim with plain words at the end.

> If in the long run the beliefs expressed in proletarian dictatorship are destined to be accepted by the dominant forces of the community, the only meaning of free speech is that they should be given their chance and have their way.

Holmes, *Gitlow v. New York* (dissenting opinion) (1925)

From *expressed* to *community*, all the significant words are Latinate. After that point, every word is Saxon (except *chance*, which anyway is simple). Those two passages just shown are among the best-known that Holmes wrote. The ideas they contain have been said elsewhere in many ways. These expressions of them owe their longevity mostly to their eloquence, and the movement between words of different kinds contributes to it. The flow from Latinate to Saxon allows force to be gathered and spent.

Holmes, *Natural Law* (1918)

When differences are sufficiently far reaching, we try to kill the other man rather than let him have his way. But that is perfectly consistent with admitting that, so far as appears, his grounds are just as good as ours.

Both sentences in that passage are examples of our theme. The first has some long Latinate words at the start (*differences* and *sufficiently*), then 14 Saxon words to end. The second has the same structure.

Holmes, *The Common Law* (1888)

The degree of civilization which a people has reached, no doubt, is marked by their anxiety to do as they would be done by.

Holmes, *Natural Law* (1918)

No doubt behind these legal rights is the fighting will of the subject to maintain them, and the spread of his emotions to the general rules by which they are maintained; but that does not seem to me the same thing as the supposed *a priori* discernment of a duty or the assertion of a preexisting right. A dog will fight for his bone.

Holmes, letter to Harold Laski (1921)

I don't believe in the infinite importance of man – I see no reason to believe that a shudder could go through the sky if the whole ant heap were kerosened.

These last two examples both end with a run of Saxon words that stand out in contrast to the Latinate flavor of what came before. (They also both end in animal metaphors, for which Holmes had a deft touch.) The passages show again how the flow of diction can follow the sense of the words. The higher and more pompous idea is put in words that came into English from Latin (*a priori discernment, infinite importance*). The truth that follows is put mostly in older and simpler words (*dog, fight, bone, shudder, sky, ant, heap*); *kerosene* is from Greek, but it now has some of the easy visual qualities of a Saxon word.

We see, then, that Holmes and Lincoln have entirely different styles and voices, but both make use of the same principles of alternation.

6. *Burke*. Edmund Burke is often regarded as the greatest British statesman of the 18th century. As usual, greatness in that sort of reputation goes along with an equivalent mastery of language. Burke's style can seem ornate to the modern ear, but he was a gifted prose stylist. He knew the value of finishing off a Latinate sequence with short words and especially with Saxon ones. He flies the plane and then lands it.

I do not enter into these metaphysical distinctions; I hate the very sound of them.

Burke, *Speech on American Taxation* (1774)

It is not what a lawyer tells me I may do; but what humanity, reason, and justice, tell me I ought to do.

Burke, *Second Speech on Conciliation with America* (1775)

Taxing is an easy business. Any projector can contrive new impositions, any bungler can add to the old.

Burke, *Speech on the Independence of Parliament* (1780)

Example is the school of mankind, and they will learn at no other.

Burke, *Letters on a Regicide Peace* (1796)

When I see in any of these detached gentlemen of our times the angelic purity, power, and beneficence, I shall admit them to be angels. In the meantime, we are born only to be men. We shall do enough if we form ourselves to be good ones.

Burke, *Thoughts on the Cause of the Present Discontents* (1770)

This last passage follows a pattern that we have seen several times: movement to Saxon words that follows the meaning of the claim. Burke is countering an idea that he does not believe. He states the false and inflated vision in Latinate words, the true one in Saxon words.

7. *Henry*. For more examples we might choose from many writers and speakers. A representative case is Patrick

Henry, the first post-colonial governor of Virginia and one of the most significant figures in the oratorical history of the American Revolution and founding. "Give me liberty or give me death" is known to all, so we might consider a few other uses he made of our theme: the use of a Saxon ending to give relief from a more Latinate sentence, or (if you prefer) the use of a Latinate sentence to set up a Saxon finish and make it stand out.

Henry, Speech at Second
Virginia Convention (1775)

If we mean not basely to abandon the noble struggle in which we have been so long engaged, and which we have pledged ourselves never to abandon until the glorious object of our contest shall be obtained, we must fight! I repeat it, sir, we must fight!

Henry, Speech at Virginia
Ratifying Convention (1788)

I conceive it my duty, if this government is adopted before it is amended, to go home.

Henry, Speech at Virginia
Ratifying Convention (1788)

I believe, sir, that a previous ratification of a system notoriously and confessedly defective will endanger our riches, our liberty, our all.

8. *Wollstonecraft*. Mary Wollstonecraft, an early feminist, made use of a pattern in which a false or despised thing is described in longer Latinate words; then the hard or true result, or alternative, is said in Saxon or other short words that end the sentence.

Wollstonecraft, *A Vindication
of the Rights of Woman* (1792)

Men, in general, seem to employ their reason to justify prejudices, which they have imbibed, they cannot trace how, rather than to root them out.

Wollstonecraft, *A Vindication
of the Rights of Woman* (1792)

Tyrants and sensualists are in the right when they endeavor to keep women in the dark, because the former only want slaves, and the latter a play-thing.

Wollstonecraft, *A Vindication
of the Rights of Woman* (1792)

And if then women do not resign the arbitrary power of beauty – they will prove that they have less mind than man.

9. *Negations and endings.* The Saxon finish can add a stark quality to a phrase, and so is especially useful for adding negation, finality, or other such points contrary to ideas expressed in bigger words. As we've seen, the come-down in register makes the ending sound decisive. Some more explicit examples:

> Diseases desperate grown
> By desperate appliance are relieved,
> Or not at all.

Hamlet 4, 3

The notice which you have been pleased to take of my labors, had it been early, had been kind; but it has been delayed till I am indifferent, and cannot enjoy it; till I am solitary, and cannot impart it; till I am known, and do not want it.

Johnson, letter to Lord Chesterfield (1755)

Inaction is followed by stagnation. Stagnation is followed by pestilence and pestilence is followed by death.

Douglass, *Self-Made Men* (1859)

You have made a monstrous charge against me; direct, distinct, public. You are bound to prove it as directly, as distinctly, or publicly; – or to own you can't.

Newman, *Mr. Kingsley and Dr. Newman: A Correspondence* (1864)

Such, stated of course in the most general terms, is the religion of which I take "Liberty, Equality, Fraternity" to be the creed. I do not believe it.

Stephen, *Liberty, Equality, Fraternity* (1873)

Our natural dispositions may be good; but we have been badly brought up, and are full of anti-social personal ambitions and prejudices and snobberies. Had we not better teach our children to be better citizens than ourselves? We are not doing that at present. The Russians are. That is my last word. Think over it.

Shaw, *The Apple Cart* (preface) (1928)

Chapter Three

THE LATINATE FINISH
AND VARIATIONS

We have seen some effects that can be produced by ending a Latinate sentence with Saxon words. Now consider the reverse: starting a sentence with Saxon words, then shifting to longer Latinate ones.

1. *The King James Bible.* A frequent product of this pattern is a sense of compression released. Moving from Saxon to Latinate words makes the first part of a sentence feel compact, the rest expansive. The last part thus gains a kind of push.

Judg. 10:14

Go and cry unto the gods which ye have chosen; let them deliver you in the time of your tribulation.

Prov. 10:29

The way of the Lord is strength to the upright: but destruction shall be to the workers of iniquity.

In that last case the good and the strong are described in simple words. The long words are reserved for the villains. We will see this pattern recur.

Dan. 4:3

How great are his signs! and how mighty are his wonders! his kingdom is an everlasting kingdom, and his dominion is from generation to generation.

These sentences go from a tight start to a finish that flows freely and gains in height. The result can be a feeling of increasing grandeur, like passing from a low ceiling into a room with a higher one.

2. *Shakespeare.* Let's consider what this pattern looked like in Shakespeare, who, as we saw earlier, would often choose a style of word that matches the substance.

I were better to be eaten to death with a rust than   *2 Henry IV*, 1, 2
to be scoured to nothing with perpetual motion.

The stationary idea is expressed with words that sit still –
the short and solid kind. The idea of motion is expressed
in words with motion in them – long words, and words
that have a cadence we will revisit later in the book.

This England never did, nor never shall,   *King John*, 5, 7
Lie at the proud foot of a conqueror.

The first words are simple. They establish strength and
resolution, and they pull back the bow. The Latinate
words (*proud, conqueror*), especially the last, then go forward to describe what is inflated and despicable. (Compare the second Biblical passage shown a moment ago.)

       Yet I'll not shed her blood;   *Othello*, 5, 3
Nor scar that whiter skin of hers than snow,
And smooth as monumental alabaster.

The words to describe the purity of the beauty are simple
and themselves pure. Then the smoothness – a different
kind of beauty – is described in words that themselves
turn long and mellifluous.

3. *Lincoln*. Lincoln's frequent goal evidently was to
speak to all capacities of his listeners. He would use
Saxon words to create feeling, make a claim personal,
and convey action. He would use Latinate words to connect the claim to principles and ideals.

I insist that if there is ANY THING which it is the   Lincoln, speech at Peoria
duty of the WHOLE PEOPLE to never entrust to   (1854)
any hands but their own, that thing is the preser-
vation and perpetuity of their own liberties and
institutions.

Lincoln didn't like to write a whole sentence that entirely
resembled the second half of the one just shown. He

preferred it to come with another half – there the first part, consisting of words that are simple and largely Saxon.

Lincoln, debate with Stephen
Douglas at Springfield (1858)

Did we brave all then to falter now – now, when that same enemy is wavering, dissevered, and belligerent?

He starts with simple words of feeling, and reserves the longer and weaker words to describe the adversary – a familiar pattern.

An example from Lincoln's last public speech, in which he considered a question put to him about the legal status of the seceding states:

Lincoln, speech at
Washington, D.C. (1865)

Whatever it may hereafter become, that question is bad, as the basis of a controversy, and good for nothing at all – a merely pernicious abstraction.

It is the usual style of Lincoln: a mix of simplicity (the question is "bad" and "good for nothing at all") with more ambitious wording. He describes the abstraction in words that themselves are abstract, the better to make it seem remote. The last two phrases in the sentence amount to restatements of the same idea in easy Saxon words and then in demanding Latinate ones. Soon we will see other uses Lincoln made of this pairing.

4. *Churchill.* Churchill had a knack, as we have seen, for movement between high and low language. The Latinate finish to a plainer sentence was one of his trademark effects.

Churchill, speech in the
House of Commons (1940)

You ask, what is our policy? I can say: It is to wage war, by sea, land, and air, with all our might and with all the strength that God can give us; to wage war against a monstrous tyranny, never surpassed in the dark and lamentable catalogue of human crime. That is our policy.

What *we* will do is stated in the simplest conceivable language: 24 words in a row of one syllable apiece, every one of them at least partly Germanic. What we are fighting *against* is stated in the opposite way: of the last 13 words of the main sentence, more than half are Latinate, and they create a sense of height and climax. The longer words also allow him to end with a flourish for the ear.

Look at the similar structure of this passage from a speech he gave a few weeks later:

> The whole root and core and brain of the British Army, on which and around which we were to build, and are to build, the great British Armies in the later years of the war, seemed about to perish upon the field or to be led into an ignominious and starving captivity.

Churchill, speech in the House of Commons (1940)

The good guys are depicted in short and sturdy words. The disastrous threat they faced is depicted in long and appalling ones. One more:

> The rights of the weak are trampled down. The grand freedoms of which the President of the United States has spoken so movingly are spurned and chained. The whole stature of man, his genius, his initiative, and his nobility, is ground down under systems of mechanical barbarism and of organized and scheduled terror.

Churchill, speech to the United States (1941)

This passage restates a similar idea in each of three sentences. First it is said in simple Saxon words. Then it is said with a mix of Saxon and Latinate words. The finale describes the evil in a run of long Latinate words that fill the mouth and take some time to say. Those properties make the words splendid for vituperation. The mounting height of the language gives the end a climactic sound.

5. *Latinate words in the middle.* We've seen simple patterns in which a sentence goes from Saxon to Latinate or vice

versa. Sometimes these kinds of words can be arranged in a *chiasmus* – a device in which two elements are arranged in an ABBA sequence. The sentence starts and ends with Saxon words, but gets fancy in the middle.

Prov. 16:18

Pride goeth before destruction, and an haughty spirit before a fall.

Matt. 14:14

And Jesus went forth, and saw a great multitude, and was moved with compassion toward them, and he healed their sick.

The diction climbs and then descends. *Pride* and *fall* are both Saxon, and are the outside or "A" members of the chiasmus; *destruction* and *haughty spirit* are Latinate words, and fill the "B" role. (The verse has sometimes been shortened in the popular imagination to a version just Saxon: "Pride goeth before a fall.") In the second, *multitude* and *compassion* are long words derived from French. They cause the last words – *and he healed their sick*, all Germanic – to stand out with more simplicity and finality.

Wollstonecraft, *A Vindication of the Rights of Men* (1790)

I bend with awful reverence when I enquire on what my fear is built.

Churchill, *The River War* (1899)

They may learn from it how much harder it is to build up and acquire, than to squander and cast away.

"Reverence" and "enquire" are Latinate. Everything on either side of them is Saxon. The shape of the sentence reflects the posture of the author. "Squander" is of unknown etymology, but it is of the same family by sound as *acquire*. "Build up" and "cast away" are Saxon. See how the pattern underscores the sense of Churchill's claim. The wording itself builds from simple to complex; then the sound of it is spent. Two more examples of this theme, in which Saxon words at the start and end of the sentence bracket Latinate words in the middle:

In war, Resolution. In defeat, Defiance. In victory, Magnanimity. In peace, Goodwill.

Churchill, *The Second World War* (1948)

But be the ordeal sharp or long, or both, we shall seek no terms, we shall tolerate no parley; we may show mercy – we shall ask for none.

Churchill, London radio broadcast (1940)

An extended case in which the Saxon finish, or return to the earth, goes well with the substance:

We might as well never have been born, unless it were necessary that we should be created to enable man to acquire the noble privilege of reason, the power of discerning good from evil, whilst we lie down in the dust from whence we were taken, never to rise again.

Wollstonecraft, *A Vindication of the Rights of Woman* (1792)

The middle of the sentence is full of words derived from Latin, but it ends with 19 in a row that aren't. Another in a like vein:

Mr. Casaubon had never had a strong bodily frame, and his soul was sensitive without being enthusiastic: it was too languid to thrill out of self-consciousness into passionate delight; it went on fluttering in the swampy ground where it was hatched, thinking of its wings and never flying.

Eliot, *Middlemarch* (1872)

Again the middle of the sentence is full of words derived from Latin. Again it ends with 19 in a row that aren't.

6. *Movement.* Sometimes writers combine Saxon and Latinate words in a pattern less smooth. The movement between them is back and forth, putting tension and energy into the discourse. Some examples from Shakespeare of what can be achieved by quick oscillation between complex and simple words:

What a piece of work is a man! How noble in reason, how infinite in faculty! In form and moving how express and admirable! In action how like an

Hamlet, 2, 2

Angel! in apprehension how like a god! The
beauty of the world! The paragon of animals! And
yet to me, what is this quintessence of dust?

Hamlet, 3, 1

To be, or not to be, that is the question:
Whether 'tis nobler in the mind to suffer
The slings and arrows of outrageous fortune
Or to take arms against a sea of troubles
And by opposing end them.

The angst of the substance is reflected in the push and
pull of the words: *slings and arrows* is Saxon; *outrageous*
and *fortune* both came into English from French. *Opposing* is Latinate; *end them* is Saxon. It is the method we
have seen Shakespeare use before: let the qualities of
words match what they express. These passages owe their
immortality to many features, of course, not to any one
technique. But the movement between different kinds of
words is one contributor to their success.

The same principles of movement were used by Melville in this well-known passage in which Ahab vents his
wrath at the whale that took his leg:

Melville, *Moby-Dick* (1851)

He tasks me; he heaps me; I see in him outrageous
strength, with an inscrutable malice sinewing it.
That inscrutable thing is chiefly what I hate; and
be the white whale agent, or be the white whale
principal, I will wreak that hate upon him.

He tasks me; he heaps me is simple; it creates an appetite
for relief by a longer phrase with Latinate words, which
comes next: *I see in him outrageous strength, with an inscrutable malice sinewing it.* Then more alternation, as he
repeatedly pairs Latinate and Saxon words (*outrageous
strength, inscrutable thing, whale agent, whale principal*).
The alternations get resolved in the climax – *I will wreak
that hate upon him* – which of course is entirely Saxon.

An example of the same principles put to work by
Holmes:

If the typical criminal is a degenerate, bound to swindle or to murder by as deep seated an organic necessity as that which makes the rattlesnake bite, it is idle to talk of deterring him by the classical method of imprisonment. He must be got rid of; he cannot be improved, or frightened out of his structural reaction.

Holmes, *The Path of the Law* (1897)

Notice again the constant movement between fancy Latinate words (*degenerate, organic necessity, classical method, structural reaction*) and hard Saxon words (*murder, rattlesnake bite, talk, must be got rid of*). Holmes wants to make conceptual points, but he also has a taste for keeping what he says vivid and specific, so he does both. The brutally simple words give the usual relief from complexity and abstraction. The contrast in language also causes a deflation of tone that helps Holmes deflate the subject, which is his point.

Chapter Four

CHOICE OF WORDS: SPECIAL EFFECTS

We have seen how the flow of movement from Latinate to Saxon words, or vice versa, can produce rhetorical gains. We turn now to a few more specific ways that the two kinds of words can be put to work.

1. *Churchill and the Saxon Restatement.* Some writers, and especially some orators, are fond of using the techniques we have considered to repeat themselves. They say roughly the same thing first in Saxon words and then in Latinate words (or the other way around). Of course this seems redundant if the only goal is to deliver a message. But the pattern can serve a strong rhetorical function by helping to stimulate both feeling and thought. It also gives the reader or listener a longer chance to take in the speaker's point.

Churchill often spoke in doublets of this kind; he liked to use words in complementary pairs. The two words frequently overlap, so a vigorous editor nowadays would tell him to just pick one. But often one of the words is Saxon and the other is Latinate, so they do different work even if the second doesn't seem to add much new meaning. They create a double-barreled sound and make different appeals to the reader's sensibilities. Count up the doublets in the passages that follow (the words and short phrases joined by conjunctions) and see how they work.

Churchill, speech in the House of Commons (1940)

And even if, which I do not for a moment believe, this island or a large part of it were subjugated and starving, then our Empire beyond the seas, armed and guarded by the British Fleet, would carry on the struggle, until, in God's good time, the

New World, with all its power and might, steps forth to the rescue and the liberation of the old.

We would rather see London laid in ruins and ashes than that it should be tamely and abjectly enslaved.

Churchill, London radio broadcast (1940)

Not all of these pairs involve a Saxon and a Latinate word, but many of them do. There is usually a fancier word and a plainer one: *subjugated* (fancy) and *starving* (plain), *tamely* (Saxon) and *abjectly* (Latinate); *ruins* (Latinate) and *ashes* (Saxon).

The doublets just shown can be considered miniatures of a larger pattern: an entire idea expressed twice, once in Saxon language and once in Latinate. Churchill liked to do this with whole phrases and sentences, not just pairs of words.

I say to the House as I said to ministers who have joined this government, I have nothing to offer but blood, toil, tears, and sweat. We have before us an ordeal of the most grievous kind.

Churchill, speech in the House of Commons (1940)

The second sentence amounts to Latinate restatement of the first. More often, though, Churchill would go the other way. Watch here how in each case he says something with Latinate words and then expresses about the same idea in words that are shorter, more visual, and more heavily Saxon:

I could not believe that they would allow the high purposes to which they have set themselves to be frustrated and the products of their skill and labor sunk to the bottom of the sea.

Churchill, London radio broadcast (1941)

When the designs of wicked men or the aggressive urge of mighty States dissolve over large areas the frame of civilized society, humble folk are confronted with difficulties with which they cannot cope. For them all is distorted, all is broken, even ground to pulp.

Churchill, speech at Fulton, Missouri (1946)

Churchill, remark on Truman
at Potsdam (1945)

At any rate, he is a man of immense determination. He takes no notice of delicate ground, he just plants his foot down firmly upon it.

2. *Lincoln and the Saxon restatement.* Lincoln used the same technique to engage thought and feeling – a general pattern that we glimpsed in a previous chapter.

Lincoln, "House Divided"
speech at Springfield (1858)

I do not expect the Union to be *dissolved* – I do not expect the house to *fall* – but I *do* expect it will cease to be divided. It will become *all* one thing, or *all* the other.

He makes a claim in Latinate words and then restates it in Saxon words. Then he does it again. *Union* and *dissolved* came to English from Latin; *house* and *fall* are Germanic. *Cease to be divided* is Latinate; then comes the Saxon restatement and climax: "It will become *all* one thing, or *all* the other." It sometimes seems as though Lincoln says anything of real importance twice – once in conceptual language, and then again simply. If he used Latinate words, his tendency was then to compensate.

Lincoln, "House Divided"
speech at Springfield (1858)

To meet and overthrow the power of that dynasty is the work now before all those who would prevent that consummation. That is what we have to do.

Some other examples of Lincoln using the two different families of words for restatement:

Lincoln, Second Inaugural
Address (1865)

Fondly do we hope, fervently do we pray, that this mighty scourge of war may speedily pass away.

Fondly and *hope* are Saxon. *Fervently* and *pray* are Latinate.

Lincoln, Thanksgiving
Proclamation (1863)

Intoxicated with unbroken success, we have become too self-sufficient to feel the necessity of redeeming and preserving grace, too proud to pray to the God that made us!

Notice the similarity of the substance in the last clause and the one before it.

3. *Johnson and the Saxon restatement.* Samuel Johnson (especially as recorded by Boswell) made use of the same general sort of Saxon restatement in his own style. His preferred pattern was to say something in long Latinate words and then restate it in language that was visual, often metaphorical, and usually more Saxon. Note again not just the movement from fancy and abstract words to the simple and visual kind, but the similarity in the meaning of what is said – first in one way, then in another.

> The Colonists could with no solidity argue from their not having been taxed while in their infancy, that they should not now be taxed. We do not put a calf into the plow; we wait till he is an ox.

Johnson, *Taxation no Tyranny* (draft) (1775)

> Truth will not afford sufficient food to their vanity; so they have betaken themselves to error. Truth, Sir, is a cow which will yield such people no more milk, and so they are gone to milk the bull.

Johnson, in Boswell's *Life* (1791)

> By exciting emulation and comparisons of superiority, you lay the foundation of lasting mischief; you make brothers and sisters hate each other.

Johnson, in Boswell's *Life* (1791)

4. *Others.* Some more examples of Saxon words used to restate or elaborate what has just been said in Latinate English:

> Certitude is not the test of certainty. We have been cocksure of many things that were not so.

Holmes, *Natural Law* (1918)

> You should not give way to this inglorious exultation. You are an Englishman, and you ought not to hit a man when he is down.

Sheil, speech in the House of Commons (1814)

> Believe nothing, or next to nothing, of what you read about internal affairs on the Government

Orwell, *Looking Back on the Spanish War* (1942)

side. It is all, from whatever source, party propaganda – that is to say, lies.

Chesterton, *The Appetite of Tyranny* (1915)

There is another idea in human arrangements so fundamental as to be forgotten; but now for the first time denied. It may be called the idea of reciprocity; or, in better English, of give and take.

Mill, *The British Constitution* (1826)

Talent, indeed, in such a situation there will be plenty: but what sort of talent? Not that of taking an enlarged and comprehensive view of the bearing of public measures upon the happiness of the bulk of his countrymen, for the bulk of his countrymen are nothing to him, nor to his master the parliament maker: he is not sent there to serve them and were he to serve them he would be sent there no more.

That last run of 21 monosyllables – also a chiasmus – is a thing of beauty.

5. *Setting up crude words.* Coarse or harsh language comes to be uninteresting by itself but can have good effects when it is unexpected or provides relief from a Latinate mood. It can also provide relief from pretension or delicacy in the substance of a claim. Holmes used this technique memorably. He liked to skewer pompous claims by others, and at the same time he liked to blow up linguistic balloons and then pop them. The two habits went together.

Holmes, letter to Frederick Pollock (1911)

I hope I am not growing dyspeptic in my judgments, but the worthy Bigelow strikes me as appearing in the undisguise of an ass in his later politico-economic lucubrations.

Holmes, letter to Patrick Sheehan (1912)

I said of the Roosevelt movement that it seemed characterized by a strenuous vagueness that made an atmospheric disturbance but transmitted no message. To prick the sensitive points of the social consciousness when one ought to know that the suggestion of cures is humbug, I think wicked.

> Hegel's trilogies when applied to concrete events in time may here and there furnish an amusing or even a suggestive synthesis at the hands of the original master, but applied by Berth, aided by Bergson, to transcending the concept and getting into life they make me puke.

Holmes, letter to Harold Laski (1917)

Churchill also knew how to make the most of a blunt word by setting it up or surrounding it with Latinate language that creates contrast.

> I had no idea in those days of the enormous and unquestionably helpful part that humbug plays in the social life of great peoples dwelling in a state of democratic freedom.

Churchill, *My Early Life* (1930)

> So now this bloodthirsty guttersnipe must launch his mechanized armies upon new fields of slaughter, pillage and devastation.

Churchill, London radio broadcast (1941)

A less extreme example, but the same general idea:

> Going back to first principles, vice skulks, with all its native deformity, from close investigation; but a set of shallow reasoners are always exclaiming that these arguments prove too much, and that a measure rotten at the core may be expedient.

Wollstonecraft, *A Vindication of the Rights of Woman* (1792)

6. *Latinate humor.* Humor can be produced by using Latinate words that seem big for the occasion. If the topic under discussion is too serious for humor (as will be true in one or two cases below), we at least get the pleasure of an ironic relationship between diction and substance. I do not mean to endorse this approach to wit in anything but moderation. But it's interesting to think about *why* these cases are amusing if they are. I would suggest that it's the usual principle: sparks produced by

friction. In this case it's the contrast between the fancy words used to speak about a thing and the lowly character of it, or between the refined language on the surface and the harsh judgment beneath. Some examples from Johnson:

Boswell, *Life of Johnson* (1791)

SIR ADAM. "But, Sir, in the British constitution it is surely of importance to keep up a spirit in the people, so as to preserve a balance against the crown." JOHNSON. "Sir, I perceive you are a vile Whig."

Boswell, *Life of Johnson* (1791)

Somebody quoted to him with admiration the soliloquy of an officer who had lived in the wilds of America: "Here am I, free and unrestrained, amidst the rude magnificence of nature, with the Indian woman by my side, and this gun, with which I can procure food when I want it! What more can be desired for human happiness?" "Do not allow yourself, sir," replied Johnson, "to be imposed upon by such gross absurdity. It is sad stuff; it is brutish. If a bull could speak, he might as well exclaim, 'Here am I with this cow and this grass; what being can enjoy greater felicity?'"

Boswell, *Life of Johnson* (1791)

JOHNSON. "Rousseau, Sir, is a very bad man. I would sooner sign a sentence for his transportation, than that of any felon who has gone from the Old Bailey these many years. Yes, I should like to have him work in the plantations." BOSWELL. "Sir, do you think him as bad a man as Voltaire?" JOHNSON. "Why, Sir, it is difficult to settle the proportion of iniquity between them."

George Eliot (Mary Ann Evans) is not regarded as a comic writer, but a good deal of irony and humor sometimes runs through her observations and language. Some of it makes use of our current theme.

He was a boy whom Mrs. Hackit had pronounced "stocky" (a word that etymologically, in all probability, conveys some allusion to an instrument of punishment for the refractory).

Eliot, Scenes of Clerical Life (1857)

The rooks were cawing with many-voiced monotony, apparently – by a remarkable approximation to human intelligence – finding great conversational resources in the change of weather.

Eliot, Scenes of Clerical Life (1857)

Plain women he regarded as he did the other severe facts of life, to be faced with philosophy and investigated by science.

Eliot, Middlemarch (1872)

An election is coming. Universal peace is declared, and the foxes have a sincere interest in prolonging the lives of the poultry.

Eliot, Felix Holt (1866)

Any of these lines could be rewritten with mostly Saxon words, which would drain the amusement from them. (*Poultry* is from French; *chickens* wouldn't have worked as well.)

Churchill liked to have this kind of fun.

He did not run away, he executed a strategic movement to the rear.

Churchill, speech at London (1904)

It cannot in the opinion of His Majesty's Government be classified as slavery in the extreme acceptance of the word without some risk of terminological inexactitude.

Churchill, speech in the House of Commons (1906)

So far as the argument is concerned I think we must all admit, without making any reproach in any quarter, that it has not been distinguished by the charm of novelty.

Churchill, speech in the House of Commons (1909)

At 4 o'clock this morning Hitler attacked and invaded Russia. All his usual formalities of perfidy were observed with scrupulous technique.

Churchill, London radio broadcast (1941)

Churchill, Question Time in
the House of Commons
(1952)

I am fully aware of the deep concern felt by the Honorable Member in many matters above his comprehension.

A few examples from elsewhere:

Dickens, speech at London
(1866)

He could not get on in the beginning without being a pupil under an anomalous creature called a "fireman waterman," who wore an eminently tall hat, and a perfectly unaccountable uniform, of which it might be said that if it was less adapted for one thing than another, that thing was fire.

Twain, *The Innocents Abroad*
(1869)

The counsel were eloquent, argumentative, and vindictively abusive of each other, as was characteristic and proper.

Lardner, *The Young Immigrunts*
(1920)

Shut up he explained.

7. *Extended examples*. So far we've seen short examples in which Latinate and Saxon words are mixed in various ways for various ends. Let's finish by seeing how our principles can look in a more extended setting. Here is a passage that Churchill wrote in 1918. He was discussing the position of Europe just before the start of World War I. Churchill often seemed to write as if with a gyroscope: if he veered in one stylistic direction, he would compensate in the other. Abstractions are relieved by imagery, and images are offset by abstractions; short sentences give way to long; little words call for bigger ones, and big ones for little.

Churchill, *The Great War*
(1918)

Such were the plans and compacts which underlay the civilization of Europe. All had been worked out to the minutest detail. They involved the marshalling for immediate battle of nearly twelve million men. For each of these there was a place reserved. For each there was a summons by name. The depots from which he would draw his uniform and weapons, the time-tables of the rail-

ways by which he would travel, the roads by which
he would march, the proclamations which would
inflame or inspire him, the food and munitions
he would require, the hospitals which would
receive his torn or shattered body – all were ready.
Only his grave was lacking; but graves do not take
long to dig. We know no spectacle in human history more instinct with pathos than that of these
twelve million men, busy with the cares, hopes
and joys of daily life, working in their fields or
mills, or seated these summer evenings by their
cottage doors with their wives and children about
them, making their simple plans for thrift or festival, unconscious of the fate which now drew near,
and which would exact from them their all.

He starts with a few sentences that are literal and moder-
ately abstract. Then comes *the roads by which he would
march* (short words, mostly Germanic); then *the proclamations which would inflame or inspire him* (longer words,
mostly Latinate). *Only his grave was lacking; but graves do
not take long to dig* – simple Germanic words, full of hard
sounds and easy to picture. Then *no spectacle in human
history more instinct with pathos* – five Latinate words in a
short space. They can't easily be pictured, and aren't supposed to be; it is a case of high diction giving a respite
from the brutality of what was just said, and inviting the
reader to reflect. This sets up the narrative that follows
(*busy with the cares…*), consisting of forty words almost
entirely from old English, intensely visual. *Festival* and
unconscious give a bit of Latinate relief from it; after this
little raising of the diction, the ear is ready for a last
descent: *the fate which now drew near, and which would
exact from them their all. Drew near*, not *approached*; and
he ends the sentence with the simplest Saxon word he
can find. So ends the drama of the diction as well as the
substance.

Now reconsider Lincoln's Gettysburg Address with his use of Saxon and Latinate words in mind:

Lincoln, Gettysburg Address
(1863)

Four score and seven years ago our fathers brought forth on this continent, a new nation, conceived in liberty, and dedicated to the proposition that all men are created equal. Now we are engaged in a great civil war, testing whether that nation, or any nation so conceived and so dedicated, can long endure. We are met on a great battle-field of that war. We have come to dedicate a portion of that field, as a final resting-place for those who here gave their lives that the nation might live. It is altogether fitting and proper that we should do this.

But, in a larger sense, we can not dedicate – we can not consecrate – we can not hallow, this ground. The brave men, living and dead, who struggled here have consecrated it, far above our poor power to add or detract. The world will little note, nor long remember, what we say here, but it can never forget what they did here. It is for us the living, rather, to be dedicated here to the unfinished work which they who fought here have thus far so nobly advanced. It is rather for us to be here dedicated to the great task remaining before us – that from these honored dead we take increased devotion to that cause for which they gave the last full measure of devotion – that we here highly resolve that these dead shall not have died in vain – that this nation, under God, shall have a new birth of freedom – and that government of the people, by the people, for the people, shall not perish from the earth.

The speech is often considered a leading specimen of Saxon prose. By one count, which my own confirms at least roughly (I have no wish to quibble), its 267 words contain just 32 of Latinate origin. Yet the Latinate words are essential to the sound as well as the substance. Read through them and see: continent, nation, conceive, liberty, dedicate, proposition, create, equal, engaged, civil, endure, portion, final, proper, consecrate, add, detract, remember, advance, remain, honored, increased, devotion, measure, resolve, vain, government, people, perish. Anyone familiar with the speech would recognize it from those words alone.

The beauty and power of Lincoln's wording lies not in a relentless use of Saxon words but in the movement between earthy language and airier words and phrases that elevate. In the first category we have *those who gave their lives that the nation might live*; *it can never forget what they did here*; *these dead shall not have died in vain.* In the second we have *the proposition that all men are created equal*; *so conceived and so dedicated*; *we cannot dedicate, we cannot consecrate*; *the last full measure of devotion.* The Saxon words create feeling and convey simplicity and sincerity. They hit home. The Latinate words evoke thought and connect the images to concepts and ideals. The sound and tone of each balances the sound and tone of the other.

Chapter Five

METONYMY

We turn from properties of words to *metonymy*, a rhetorical device in which you refer to a thing by invoking something associated with it. *The pen is mightier than the sword*, for example: the "pen" and "sword" aren't literally the point of the expression; those words are stand-ins for the activities they represent. They are metonyms. Metonymy is of interest for several reasons.

a. Metonyms can be set off against abstractions in the same way that Saxon words can be set off against Latinate words. Alternating between the specific and the general creates rhetorical vigor.

b. Metonymy can accomplish a great deal in a small space. It lets an example – perhaps a single word – encapsulate a large category.

c. Metonymy can make an abstraction more vivid and compelling. It creates an image, and so engages the imagination in some of the ways that a metaphor does.

1. *Simple examples.* Metonymy is common in the Bible.

Matt. 6:11

Give us this day our daily bread.

Matt. 27:25

Then answered all the people, and said, His blood be on us, and on our children.

John 1:14

And the Word was made flesh, and dwelt among us.

Bread, blood, and *flesh* are all metonyms. In each case they offer a physical stand-in for something larger or more abstract. They are, indeed, examples of a particular form of metonymy known as synecdoche (pronounced sin-*eck*-duh-kee, a little like the city of Schenectady, New York) – the use of a part to suggest the whole.

Doctor Swift says one man in armor will beat ten men in their shirts. Shirt is synecdoche. Part for the whole.

Joyce, *Ulysses* (1922)

Since many consider every case of synecdoche to also be a case of metonymy, we will stick with the latter term.

No man uses figures of speech with more propriety because he knows that one figure is called a metonymy and another a synecdoche.

Macaulay, *Francis Bacon* (1837)

Turning back to simple examples, here are two from Shakespeare:

Friends, Romans, countrymen, lend me your ears.

Julius Cæsar, 3, 2

Uneasy lies the head that wears a crown.

2 *Henry IV*, 3, 1

Lincoln, of course, also made skillful use of metonymy. Below are three cases in which he uses the device to speak of slavery and slaves, and so to make the subject more vivid and immediate.

Familiarize yourselves with the chains of bondage and you prepare your own limbs to wear them.

Lincoln, speech at Edwardsville (1858)

In the right to eat the bread, without the leave of anybody else, which his own hand earns, he is my equal, and the equal of Judge Douglas, and the equal of every living man.

Lincoln, debate with Stephen Douglas at Ottawa (1858)

Yet, if God wills that [the war] continue until all the wealth piled by the bondsman's two hundred and fifty years of unrequited toil shall be sunk, and until every drop of blood drawn with the lash shall be paid by another drawn with the sword, as was said three thousand years ago, so still it must be said, "The judgments of the Lord are true and righteous altogether."

Lincoln, Second Inaugural Address (1865)

Chains, *bread*, and *blood/lash* are metonyms: specific images used to capture a larger category.

Pairs of metonyms can capture a range of situations in a few words.

Richardson, *Clarissa* (1748)

What friends does prosperity make! What enemies adversity! It always was, and always will be so, in every state of life, from the throne to the cottage.

Butler, *The Way of All Flesh* (1902)

Trace a man's career from his cradle to his grave and mark how Fortune has treated him. You will find that when he is once dead she can for the most part be vindicated from the charge of any but very superficial fickleness.

Cobbett, *Important Considerations for the People of This Kingdom* (1803)

From the church to the cell, from the castle to the cottage; no state of life, however lofty or however humble, escaped their rapacious assaults.

2. *Multiple metonyms.* Sets of metonyms – multiple pairs, or longer lists – can create a stream of imagery and a compendious feel.

Burke, *Speech on the Power of Juries in Prosecutions for Libels* (1771)

What does a juror say to a judge when he refuses his opinion upon a question of judicature? You are so corrupt, that I should consider myself a partaker of your crime, were I to be guided by your opinion; or you are so grossly ignorant, that I, fresh from my bounds, from my plough, my counter, or my loom, am fit to direct you in your profession.

Some of the items in the next illustrations might simply be considered examples rather than metonyms; the gain in concreteness works in a similar way for rhetorical purposes:

Macaulay, *The History of England* (1855)

The evil was felt daily and hourly in almost every place and by almost every class, in the dairy and on the threshing floor, by the anvil and by the loom, on the billows of the ocean and in the depths of the mine.

This is the Court of Chancery, which has its decaying houses and its blighted lands in every shire, which has its worn-out lunatic in every madhouse and its dead in every churchyard, which has its ruined suitor with his slipshod heels and threadbare dress borrowing and begging through the round of every man's acquaintance, which gives to monied might the means abundantly of wearying out the right, which so exhausts finances, patience, courage, hope, so overthrows the brain and breaks the heart, that there is not an honorable man among its practitioners who would not give – who does not often give – the warning, "Suffer any wrong that can be done you rather than come here!"

Dickens, Bleak House (1853)

3. *Classic families.* Some ideas are represented by metonyms notably often. Frequent uses involve subjects severe and disagreeable, such as tortures, prison, and execution. Metonymy makes them vivid.

A "struggle for ascendency" does not mean mere argument. It means reiterated and varied assertion persisted in, in the face of the wheel, the stake, and the gallows, as well as in the face of contradiction.

Stephen, Liberty, Equality, Fraternity (1873)

Likewise the martial metonym, or the metonym based on weapons:

The manner in which the Convention had decided the question of ecclesiastical polity had not been more offensive to the Bishops themselves than to those fiery Covenanters who had long, in defiance of sword and carbine, boot and gibbet, worshipped their Maker after their own fashion in caverns and on mountain tops.

Macaulay, The History of England (1855)

We were the first, in this ancient island, to draw the sword against tyranny.

Churchill, speech at London (1945)

Or the metonym to refer to death and decay:

Sterling, letter to Thomas
Carlyle (1843)

Only it is labor that I thoroughly like; and which keeps the maggots out of one's brain, until their time.

Melville, *Pierre* (1852)

Is there then all this work to one book, which shall be read in a very few hours; and, far more frequently, utterly skipped in one second; and which, in the end, whatever it be, must undoubtedly go to the worms?

4. *Restatement.* Now some effects created by combining metonymy with abstraction and letting one offset the other. We will see similarities to the ways that Saxon and Latinate words can be varied, and sometimes the two types of variation are used at the same time. The metonym is expressed in Saxon words, the nearby abstraction in Latinate words.

We start with patterns in which a metonym restates an abstract version of the same point that comes before or afterwards. An example where the metonym comes first, then a similar idea in different words:

Hamlet, I, 3

Give every man thy ear, but few thy voice;
Take each man's censure, but reserve thy judgment.

Now the other way around: the abstraction comes first, followed by a metonym that expresses the idea more memorably:

Williams, speech at New York
Ratifying Convention (1788)

The command of the revenues of a state gives the command of everything in it. He that hath the purse will have the sword.

Bagehot, *The Waverley Novels*
(1858)

In truth, poverty is an anomaly to rich people; it is very difficult to make out why people who want dinner do not ring the bell.

Judging the use of a metonym often means looking at more than just the image itself. The entire effect of the device depends on the relationship between the image and what lies near it. It's like a piece of music in which the effect is owed not to a chord but to the movement from one chord to another.

5. *Deflation*. A metonym, by offering a picture of some thing in the world, can create a feeling of hard truth. That makes it a good device for letting the air out of an abstraction.

> The prattling about the rights of men will not be accepted in payment for a biscuit or a pound of gunpowder.

Burke, *Reflections on the Revolution in France* (1790)

> If he does really think that there is no distinction between virtue and vice, why, Sir, when he leaves our houses let us count our spoons.

Johnson, in Boswell's *Life* (1791)

> It is a piece of idle sentimentality that truth, merely as truth, has any inherent power denied to error, of prevailing against the dungeon and the stake.

Mill, *On Liberty* (1869)

In each case the move from abstract language to metonymy follows the sense of the claim. The speaker means to throw ridicule or cold water onto an idea. The idea is expressed in the abstract. The objection is expressed in a metonym. Elsewhere we've seen writers use a move from Latinate to Saxon words for the same purpose. The technique here is parallel; and as those examples show, the two methods can be easily combined.

6. *Inflation*. The same alternation of abstract and concrete can be used for a purpose roughly opposite to the one just shown. The down-to-earth character of a metonym may suggest, in addition to hard reality, mere practicality. A metonym can make an abstraction seem more favorable or prominent; the small metonym causes the larger thing to seem larger still by contrast.

Thoreau, *Walden* (1854)

It is worth the expense of youthful days and costly hours, if you learn only some words of an ancient language, which are raised out of the trivialness of the street, to be perpetual suggestions and provocations.

Churchill, London radio broadcast (1941)

What a triumph the life of these battered cities is, over the worst that fire and bomb can do.

In the example from Thoreau, the metonym (*street*) reinforces the triviality that is being claimed and creates a contrast with what the words can be in the mind (*suggestions and provocations*). The sentence from Churchill reverses the order but is a similar pattern. The abstractions – *triumph* and *life* – are elevated by their distance from the earthly threats described by the metonyms.

O'Connell, speech at Mullaghmast (1843)

I admit there is the force of a law, because it has been supported by the policeman's truncheon, by the soldier's bayonet, and by the horseman's sword; because it is supported by the courts of law and those who have power to adjudicate in them; but I say solemnly, it is not supported by constitutional right.

O'Connell wants to heap contempt on the law, so he uses metonyms to describe its underpinnings (*truncheon, bayonet,* and *sword*). They increase the contrast with the support that the laws should have but don't (*constitutional right*). The abstraction gains status by comparison.

When movement from the concrete to the abstract creates elevation, the purpose need not be to belittle the first half of the movement. The particular instance may already have great dignity, and then be tied to the hopes or ideals that follow.

Ps. 24:4

He that hath clean hands, and a pure heart; who hath not lifted up his soul unto vanity, nor sworn deceitfully.

He shall receive the blessing from the Lord,
and righteousness from the God of his salvation.

That example also illustrates movement from Saxon to
Latinate words. Here is another; we saw it in the first
chapter as an example of Saxon-to-Latinate restatement,
but can view it again as an instance of the pattern we are
considering now:

> I say to the House as I said to ministers who have
> joined this government, I have nothing to offer
> but blood, toil, tears, and sweat. We have before us
> an ordeal of the most grievous kind.

Churchill, speech in the
House of Commons (1940)

7. *Descent or ascent.* An appealing rhetorical pattern
traces a descent that starts with abstraction, moves to
example, and ends in metonymy. The picturesque image
at the end clinches the speaker's case.

> Mankind seems, at moments, the mere puppet of
> those laws of natural selection, and competition
> of species, of which we have heard so much of
> late; and, to give a single instance, the seeming
> waste, of human thought, of human agony, of
> human power, seems but another instance of that
> inscrutable prodigality of nature, by which, of a
> thousand acorns dropping to the ground, but one
> shall become the thing it can become, and grow
> into a builder oak, the rest be craunched up by the
> nearest swine.

Kingsley, *The Limits of Exact
Science as Applied to History*
(1860)

> GOLDSMITH. "It is for fear of something that he
> has resolved to kill himself; and will not that
> timid disposition restrain him?" JOHNSON. "It
> does not signify that the fear of something made
> him resolve; it is upon the state of his mind, after
> the resolution is taken, that I argue. Suppose a
> man, either from fear, or pride, or conscience, or
> whatever motive, has resolved to kill himself;

Johnson, in Boswell's *Life*
(1791)

when once the resolution is taken, he has nothing
to fear. He may then go and take the King of Prus-
sia by the nose, at the head of his army."

Holmes's most influential judicial statement used
metonymy to express the idea that the Constitution
doesn't require governments to adhere to libertarian
economic ideas:

Holmes, *Lochner v. New York*
(dissenting opinion) (1905)

The liberty of the citizen to do as he likes so long
as he does not interfere with the liberty of others
to do the same, which has been a shibboleth for
some well known writers, is interfered with by
school laws, by the Post Office, by every state or
municipal institution which takes his money for
purposes thought desirable, whether he likes it or
not. The Fourteenth Amendment does not enact
Mr. Herbert Spencer's Social Statics.

He starts with abstractions, then moves to examples and
finishes with a metonym: Spencer's book, which stands
in for the family of ideas with which the book was
associated.

The reverse pattern – ascension – is also possible:
starting with metonyms and climbing from them into
abstractions.

Shaw, *Man and Superman*
(1903)

The plague, the famine, the earthquake, the tem-
pest were too spasmodic in their action; the tiger
and crocodile were too easily satiated and not
cruel enough: something more constantly, more
ruthlessly, more ingeniously destructive was
needed; and that something was Man, the inven-
tor of the rack, the stake, the gallows, and the elec-
trocutor; of the sword and gun; above all, of
justice, duty, patriotism and all the other isms by
which even those who are clever enough to be
humanely disposed are persuaded to become the
most destructive of all the destroyers.

8. *Dramatic effect.* Sometimes alternation just puts life into rhetoric without more pointed results. There is movement between general and specific, air and earth, abstraction and metonymy. Each end of the polarity sets off the other.

> It is beyond doubt, that, under the terror of the bayonet, and the lamp-post, and the torch to their houses, they are obliged to adopt all the crude and desperate measures suggested by clubs composed of a monstrous medley of all conditions, tongues, and nations.

Burke, *Reflections on the Revolution in France* (1790)

Holmes often liked to write this way, putting little particulars and images alongside large points and abstractions.

> It is one thing to utter a happy phrase from a protected cloister; another to think under fire – to think for action upon which great interests depend. The most powerful men are apt to go into the melee and fall or come out generals. The great problems are questions of here and now. Questions of here and now occupy nine hundred and ninety-nine thousandths of the ability of the world; and when the now has passed and has given place to another now, the heads and hands that built the organic structure of society are forgotten from the speech of their fellows and live only in the tissue of their work.

Holmes, *George Otis Shattuck* (1897)

The Irish orator Henry Grattan had the same habit.

> With regard to the liberties of America, which were inseparable from ours, I will suppose this gentleman to have been an enemy decided and unreserved; that he voted against her liberty, and voted, moreover, for an address to send 4,000 Irish troops to cut the throats of the Americans; that he called these butchers "armed negotiators,"

Grattan, speech in the Irish Parliament (1783)

54 ◆ CHAPTER FIVE

and stood with a metaphor in his mouth, and a
bribe in his pocket, a champion against the rights
of America, the only hope of Ireland, and the only
refuge of the liberties of mankind.

Grattan, speech in the Irish
Parliament (1780)

I never will be satisfied so long as the meanest cot-
tager in Ireland has a link of the British chain
clanking to his rags: he may be naked, he shall not
be in iron; and I do see the time is at hand, the
spirit is gone forth, the declaration is planted and
though great men should apostatize, yet the cause
will live; and though the public speaker should
die, yet the immortal fire shall outlast the organ
which conveyed it, and the breath of liberty, like
the word of the holy man, will not die with the
prophet but survive him.

These writers all scatter metonyms among abstractions.
The climb and fall between those poles helps give their
speech and writing a sense of oscillation and heat. Compare it to an orchestral passage with a lot of movement
between softer and louder. The movement arrests the
attention. Of course it is rare for anyone, then or now, to
desire quite such intensity. But it's useful to see how it
has been produced when needed.

Chapter Six

HYPERBOLE

Hyperbole is the rhetorical use of exaggeration. Johnson's dictionary offered this definition: "A figure in rhetoric by which any thing is increased or diminished beyond the exact truth: as, he runs faster than lightning." The etymology of the word is Greek: from hyper, meaning "over," and ballein, meaning "throw." Hyperbole thus means overthrowing: a claim that goes too far. To bring the idea closer to the theory of this book, hyperbole provides a kind of relief from the literal; it amounts to alternation between the plain and accurate on the one hand and the nonliteral on the other.

Exaggeration might normally be expected to reduce a speaker's credibility. Hyperbole, properly used, avoids that problem because it is not offered in earnest. The audience knows that you know that they know that you're exaggerating; nobody is deceived or meant to be deceived. Hyperbole thus is effective only to the extent that it is obvious. One should exaggerate greatly or not at all.

"Don't say anything against my honour!" enjoined Jude hotly, standing up. "I'd marry the W— of Babylon rather than do anything dishonourable! No reflection on you, my dear. It is a mere rhetorical figure – what they call in the books, hyperbole."

Hardy, *Jude the Obscure* (1895)

Some more specific functions of hyperbole:

a. A departure from literalism gets the attention of the audience. Something surprising has been said.

b. Hyperbole can convey how the truth feels or seems, as distinct from what it may be in fact.

c. The departure from literalism involves the audience by inviting unspoken dialogue. The listener perceives that what the speaker said wasn't true, and also that the speaker knows it. They understand each other with a nod of the head.

d. Hyperbole often creates humor because it involves absurd proportions. (So we will see a lot of Dickens and Twain in this chapter.)

e. Open exaggeration may drag the audience a little closer to the speaker's strong opinion than a literal statement would. The effect can resemble the way an overly extravagant demand in a negotiation can pull a party in that direction, even if not all the way.

f. Hyperbole can be considered another form of rhetorical expansion, a bit analogous to the use of Latinate words or long sentences. Its consequences are different, but it is another way to create contrast – this time against the literal sound of ordinary speech – and thus to seize attention and produce energy.

1. *Classic species of hyperbole.* Hyperbole throws its subject into an extreme light. Some patterns for this purpose are traditional and familiar. One of them might be considered worldly hyperbole: look everywhere and you will find no case as extreme as this.

Walpole, letter to H.S.Conway (1772)

Exercise is the worst thing in the world, and as bad an invention as gunpowder.

de Quincey, *Confessions of an English Opium Eater* (1821)

It was a Sunday afternoon, wet and cheerless: and a duller spectacle this earth of ours has not to show than a rainy Sunday in London.

Chesterton, *William Morris and His School* (1903)

In all created nature there is not, perhaps, anything so completely ugly as a pillar-box.

Conrad, *The Shadow Line* (1917)

Captain Giles' appearance excluding the suspicion of mere sly malice, I came to the conclusion that he was simply the most tactless idiot on earth.

Lest these examples all seem unflattering to their subjects:

There were two reasons why all these fancies should float through the mind in the streets of this especial town of Belfort. First of all, it lies close upon the boundary of France and Germany, and boundaries are the most beautiful things in the world.

Chesterton, *The Lion* (1909)

Or temporal hyperbole: ours is the most extreme case ever.

I beg pardon for having detained you so long; but your Lordships will be so good as to observe that no business ever was covered with more folds of iniquitous artifice than this which is now brought before you.

Burke, speech in the impeachment of Warren Hastings (1788)

The majority of the House more justly regarded him as the falsest, the most malignant and the most impudent being that had ever disgraced the human form.

Macaulay, *The History of England* (1848)

When crushed, sage brush emits an odor which isn't exactly magnolia and equally isn't exactly polecat but is a sort of compromise between the two. It looks a good deal like grease-wood, and is the ugliest plant that was ever conceived of.

Twain, letter to his mother (1861)

With *never*.

She writhes under her life. A woman more angry, passionate, reckless, and revengeful never lived.

Dickens, *Little Dorrit* (1857)

Why, this is a monstrous sort of talk about the Constitution of the United States! There has never been as outlandish or lawless a doctrine from the mouth of any respectable man on earth.

Lincoln, debate with Stephen Douglas at Alton (1858)

With *since*.

He no sooner formed this resolution than he saluted Miss Squeers and the friend with great gallantry, and drawing a chair to the tea-table,

Dickens, *Nicholas Nickleby* (1839)

began to make himself more at home than in all probability an usher has ever done in his employer's house since ushers were first invented.

Lincoln, letter to H.C. Whitney (1855)

Your note containing election news is received; and for which I thank you. It is all of no use, however. Logan is worse beaten than any other man ever was since elections were invented – beaten more than twelve hundred in this county.

The *first*.

Burke, speech in the impeachment of Warren Hastings (1788)

My Lords, this is the first man, I believe, that ever took credit for his sincerity from his breach of his promises.

Chesterton, *Demagogues and Mystagogues* (1915)

So far from this being a time in which things are praised because they are popular, the truth is that this is the first time, perhaps, in the whole history of the world in which things can be praised because they are unpopular.

The *last*.

Wells, *An Englishman Looks at the World* (1914)

Politicians and statesmen, being the last people in the world to notice what is going on in it, are making no attempt whatever to re-adapt this hugely growing floating population of delocalized people to the public service.

A case of hyperbole can also be made extreme in its class – the ultimate example of whatever it is.

Hazlitt, *On Living to One's Self* (1821)

There is not a more mean, stupid, dastardly, pitiful, selfish, spiteful, envious, ungrateful animal than the Public.

Chesterton, *Christmas* (1915)

There is no more dangerous or disgusting habit than that of celebrating Christmas before it comes, as I am doing in this article.

The *if/then* construction:

Britain, with an army to enforce her tyranny, has declared that she has a right "to BIND us in ALL CASES WHATSOEVER," and if being bound in that manner is not slavery, then is there not such a thing as slavery upon earth.

Paine, *The American Crisis* (1783)

If you desert me, Nelly, there is no such thing as friendship in the world.

Shaw, *The Irrational Knot* (1905)

2. *Exaggeration of extent.* Sometimes hyperbole is achieved not by awarding an extreme distinction to the subject but just by enlarging it. The simplest cases increase the numbers at stake.

The prosperous patronage with which he said it, made him look twice as big as he was, and four times as offensive.

Dickens, *A Tale of Two Cities* (1859)

We closed our thirteenth mile of weary, round-about marching, and emerged upon the sea-shore abreast the ships, with our usual escort of fifteen hundred Piraean dogs howling at our heels.

Twain, *The Innocents Abroad* (1869)

Or the hyperbole can, without numbers, just run further in the direction of the truth than the truth would go.

And for Mark Antony, think not of him,
For he can do no more than Cæsar's arm
When Cæsar's head is off.

Julius Cæsar, 2, 1

I tell you what, sir; there are a hundred fathers, within a circuit of five miles from this place; well off; good, rich, substantial men; who would gladly give their daughters, and their own ears with them, to that very man yonder, ape and mummy as he looks.

Dickens, *Nicholas Nickleby* (1839)

Dickens, *Little Dorrit* (1857)

Why, I'd as soon have a spit put through me, and be stuck upon a card in a collection of beetles, as lead the life I have been leading here.

Twain, *Roughing It* (1872)

Nothing in this world is palled in such impenetrable obscurity as a U.S. Treasury Comptroller's understanding. The very fires of the hereafter could get up nothing more than a fitful glimmer in it.

A species of this genus is the overgeneralization, in which all – the whole world – is used to refer to something less than all.

John 12:19

The Pharisees therefore said among themselves, Perceive ye how ye prevail nothing? behold, the world is gone after him.

Thackeray, *Vanity Fair* (1848)

Who has not remarked the readiness with which the closest of friends and honestest of men suspect and accuse each other of cheating when they fall out on money matters? Everybody does it. Everybody is right, I suppose, and the world is a rogue.

3. *The hyperbolic counterfactual.* In which an exaggerated prediction is offered: if they could have done X, they would have, etc.

Dickens, *Nicholas Nickleby* (1839)

The resolution was, of course, carried with loud acclamations, every man holding up both hands in favour of it, as he would in his enthusiasm have held up both legs also, if he could have conveniently accomplished it.

Dickens, *David Copperfield* (1850)

To everybody in succession, Captain Hopkins said: "Have you read it?" – "No." – "Would you like to hear it read?" If he weakly showed the least disposition to hear it, Captain Hopkins, in a loud sonorous voice, gave him every word of it. The

Captain would have read it twenty thousand
times, if twenty thousand people would have
heard him, one by one.

…and a brain, and a heart, and a soul in him, gentlemen, which had made Steelkilt Charlemagne,
had he been born son to Charlemagne's father.

Melville, *Moby-Dick* (1851)

4. *Additions.* The comic effect of hyperbole can be
increased with tokens of faux earnestness. The assurances
may be explicit, as when offering words to make the
claim seem to follow from reflection (*after many years of
consideration* in this first case):

The Master, upon this, put his hand underneath
the skirts of his coat, and brought out his flute in
three pieces, which he screwed together, and began
immediately to play. My impression is, after many
years of consideration, that there never can have
been anybody in the world who played worse.

Dickens, *David Copperfield*
(1850)

Or surrounding words can make the exaggeration sound
thoughtful or exact. This was a common device of
Twain's.

But if there is an eighth wonder in the world, it
must be the dwelling-houses of Naples. I honestly
believe a good majority of them are a hundred
feet high! And the solid brick walls are seven feet
through. You go up nine flights of stairs before
you get to the "first" floor. No, not nine, but there
or thereabouts.

Twain, *The Innocents Abroad*
(1869)

A dead man could get up a better legend than this
one. I don't mean a fresh dead man either; I mean
a man that's been dead weeks and weeks.

Twain, *Life on the Mississippi*
(1883)

Details can add mock verisimilitude to a hyperbolic
claim.

Irving, *Knickerbocker's History of New York* (1809)

In fact, he never gave vent to his passion until he got fairly among the Highlands of the Hudson, when he let fly whole volleys of Dutch oaths, which are said to linger to this very day among the echoes of the Dunderberg, and to give particular effect to the thunder-storms in that neighborhood.

Such details can be piled up to extend a case of ridicule, creating a result that has a family resemblance to the Homeric simile: the accumulation of specific points of comparison that go beyond the reader's needs, but that create a more vivid impression.

Dickens, *Nicholas Nickleby* (1839)

And now, there he sat, with the remains of a beard at least a week old encumbering his chin; a soiled and crumpled shirt-frill crouching, as it were, upon his breast, instead of standing boldly out; a demeanour so abashed and drooping, so despondent, and expressive of such humiliation, grief, and shame; that if the souls of forty unsubstantial housekeepers, all of whom had had their water cut off for non-payment of the rate, could have been concentrated in one body, that one body could hardly have expressed such mortification and defeat as were now expressed in the person of Mr Lillyvick the collector.

Mencken, *The Sahara of the Bozart* (1917)

He was the last bard of Dixie, at least in the legitimate line. Down there a poet is almost as rare as an oboe-player, a dry-point etcher or a metaphysician. It is, indeed, amazing to contemplate so vast a vacuity. One thinks of the interstellar spaces, of the colossal reaches of the now mythical ether. Nearly the whole of Europe could be lost in that stupendous region of fat farms, shoddy cities and paralyzed cerebrums: one could throw in France, Germany and Italy, and still have room for the British Isles. And yet, for all its size and all its wealth and all the "progress" it babbles of, it is almost as sterile, artistically, intellectually, culturally, as the Sahara Desert.

Chapter Seven

THE LENGTHS OF SENTENCES

Sentences are units of thought and of the reader's attention. Conventional guides to style often recommend that sentences average about twenty words in length, with some variation to avoid tedium. Like the advice to use Saxon words whenever you can, that advice about sentences can't quite be described as *wrong*. But good writers know more than simple advice can capture. Sometimes shorter sentences are better, sometimes longer; and great effects can be achieved by contrast between them.

1. *Variety.* Below is a comparison to illustrate the general value of contrast. I took a paragraph from a judicial opinion by Oliver Wendell Holmes and graphed the number of words in each sentence. I then did the same with a paragraph written by William Rehnquist. I chose Rehnquist as an example of a typical modern Supreme Court Justice; any number of others would have done as well. Here is a chart showing the results:

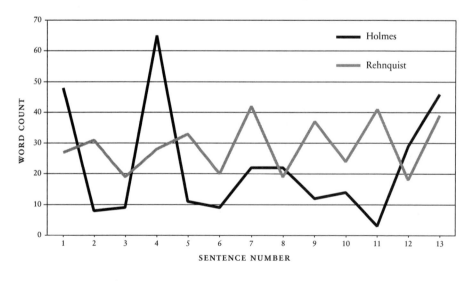

The lighter line shows the lengths of Rehnquist's sentences. They roughly alternate between about 20 and 40 words. The darker line shows the lengths of Holmes's sentences. The *averages* are similar, and both might seem to follow the standard advice about lengths of sentences. But Holmes's longest are much longer and his shortest are much shorter, and there are vertiginous climbs and drops between them. It's no accident that the line with much more variation belongs to a judge celebrated for literary ability.

The critic George Saintsbury held, in his *History of English Prose Rhythm* (1912), that "the actual mingling of short sentence and long is almost an indispensable resource for all styles." But he also warned against overdoing it – against "excessive contraction and letting out, the constant sending forth of giant and dwarf in company." His counsel was wise on both counts.

2. *Long sentences to set up short ones.* Just as short words are most striking when set against longer ones, short sentences are shown to advantage next to the longer kind. We start with cases in which a short sentence is set up by a longer one. These are modest examples of the idea; the longer sentences here are not very formidable, averaging just over forty words. But this general pattern is common in classical English rhetoric.

For myself, Sir, I do not admit the competency of South Carolina, or any other State, to prescribe my constitutional duty; or to settle, between me and the people, the validity of laws of Congress for which I have voted. I decline her umpirage.

Webster, Reply to Hayne (1830)

What plans the ministry were forming, were as unknown to the people within the city, as what the citizens were doing was unknown to the ministry; and what movements Broglio might make for the support or relief of the place, were to the citizens equally as unknown. All was mystery and hazard.

Paine, *The Rights of Man* (1791)

Burke, *Reflections on the*
Revolution in France (1790)

The military conspiracies, which are to be reme-
died by civic confederacies; the rebellious munic-
ipalities, which are to be rendered obedient by
furnishing them with the means of seducing the
very armies of the state that are to keep them in
order; all these chimeras of a monstrous and por-
tentous policy must aggravate the confusion from
which they have arisen. There must be blood.

Notice that the substance of the short sentence often has
a particular relationship to the longer one. It summa-
rizes or punctuates what has been said at more length.
We saw in early chapters the power of using short and
concrete words to restate what has already been said in a
longer and more abstract way. The idea here is parallel.

A long sentence can sometimes create enough
momentum to set up two or three short ones.

Paine, *Common Sense* (1776)

Perhaps the sentiments contained in the following
pages are not yet sufficiently fashionable to procure them general favor; a long habit of not thinking a thing wrong, gives it a superficial appearance
of being right, and raises at first a formidable out-
cry in defense of custom. But the tumult soon sub-
sides. Time makes more converts than reason.

Churchill, London radio
broadcast (1940)

Here in this strong City of Refuge which enshrines
the title-deeds of human progress and is of deep
consequence to Christian civilization; here, girt
about by the seas and oceans where the Navy
reigns; shielded from above by the prowess and
devotion of our airmen – we await undismayed the
impending assault. Perhaps it will come tonight.
Perhaps it will come next week. Perhaps it will
never come.

And here, finally, is Holmes, doing the sort of writing that
produced the steep lines on the graph shown earlier:

But when men have realized that time has upset
many fighting faiths, they may come to believe
even more than they believe the very foundations
of their own conduct that the ultimate good
desired is better reached by free trade in ideas –
that the best test of truth is the power of the
thought to get itself accepted in the competition
of the market, and that truth is the only ground
upon which their wishes safely can be carried out.
That at any rate is the theory of our Constitution.
It is an experiment, as all life is an experiment.

Holmes, *Abrams v. United
States* (dissenting opinion)
(1919)

3. *The use of short sentences to set up longer ones.* Now for
the opposite pattern: a few short sentences can create a
compression that is spent in the long one that follows.

We got in. The steps went up. The coach drove off.
The murmurs of mine hostess, not very indis-
tinctly or ambiguously pronounced, became after
a time inaudible – and now my conscience, which
the whimsical scene had for a while suspended,
beginning to give some twitches, I waited, in the
hope that some justification would be offered by
these serious persons for the seeming injustice of
their conduct.

Lamb, *Imperfect Sympathies*
(1823)

They displayed the virtues of barbarism. They
were brave and honest. The smallness of their
intelligence excused the degradation of their habits. Their ignorance secured their innocence. Yet
their eulogy must be short, for though their customs, language, and appearance vary with the districts they inhabit and the subdivisions to which
they belong, the history of all is a confused legend
of strife and misery, their natures are uniformly
cruel and thriftless, and their condition is one of
equal squalor and want.

Churchill, *The River War*
(1899)

Chesterton, *The Tyranny of
Bad Journalism* (1917)

The point about the Press is that it is not what it is
called. It is not the "popular Press." It is not the
public Press. It is not an organ of public opinion.
It is a conspiracy of a very few millionaires, all sufficiently similar in type to agree on the limits of
what this great nation (to which we belong) may
know about itself and its friends and enemies.

4. *Short sentences.* Very long and very short sentences are
not the only choices when the writer seeks variety. One
can achieve fine effects with smaller movements – say,
between sentences that are short and very short. This was
a Churchillian specialty.

Churchill, speech at
Manchester (1938)

How far, alas, do man's endeavors fall short in
practice of his inspirations! Great States and peoples have fallen away. Some have violated the faith
they had pledged. Some are seduced by intrigue,
or have yielded themselves to the cynical, short-
sighted and selfish. Many are oppressed by a sense
of isolation and weakness. Others are obviously
frightened. The Covenant has been broken. The
League has been frustrated. Over all the anxious
Governments, over all the vast masses, broods the
baleful shadow of disunity and failure. In our ears
ring the taunts of mockery and the reproach of
fiasco.

Churchill, speech in the
House of Commons (1940)

The whole of the warring nations are engaged,
not only soldiers, but the entire population, men,
women and children. The fronts are everywhere.
The trenches are dug in the towns and streets.
Every village is fortified. Every road is barred. The
front line runs through the factories. The workmen
are soldiers with different weapons but the same
courage. These are great and distinctive changes
from what many of us saw in the struggle of a
quarter of a century ago.

Both of these passages have a similar structure. Taken together they contain 18 sentences; the longest of the sentences is 22 words. Most the sentences are short and all of them are simple. But there is still some oscillation; a sentence of merely ordinary length feels refreshing after a few that are very short. Churchill was a reader of Macaulay and was influenced by him. To the examples just shown, compare this:

> Even after this event, the irresolution or dissimu-
> lation of Harley kept up the hopes of the Whigs
> during another month; and then the ruin became
> rapid and violent. The Parliament was dissolved.
> The Ministers were turned out. The Tories were
> called to office. The tide of popularity ran vio-
> lently in favour of the High Church party. That
> party, feeble in the late House of Commons, was
> now irresistible. The power which the Tories had
> thus suddenly acquired, they used with blind and
> stupid ferocity.

Macaulay, *The Life and Writings of Addison* (1843)

A series of short sentences creates a sense of rush, and so lends itself well to describing fast action, conceptual or literal.

> We have had laws. We have had blood. New trea-
> sons have been created. The Press has been shack-
> led. The Habeas Corpus Act has been suspended.
> Public meetings have been prohibited. The event
> has proved that these expedients were mere pallia-
> tives. You are at the end of your palliatives. The evil
> remains. It is more formidable than ever. What is
> to be done?

Macaulay, speech in the House of Commons (1831)

> The attack crumples. The Emirs – horse and man –
> collapse. The others turn and walk – for they will
> not run – sullenly back towards the town. The
> square starts forward. The road to the river is open.
> With dusk the water is reached, and never have

Churchill, *The River War* (1899)

victors gained a more longed-for prize. The Nile is won.

Writing or speech cannot go on too long in such a staccato way without tiring the reader, but it is effective when used sparingly. It is powerful as well as bearable precisely because it is not typical.

Short sentences lend themselves to easy combination with *anaphora*, the rhetorical device in which several sentences in a row are started the same way.

Hoar, speech in the Senate (1902)	This war, if you call it war, has gone on for three years. It will go on in some form for three hundred years, unless this policy be abandoned. You will undoubtedly have times of peace and quiet, or pretended submission. You will buy men with titles, or office, or salaries. You will intimidate cowards. You will get pretended and fawning submission. The land will smile and seem at peace. But the volcano will be there. The lava will break out again. You can never settle this thing until you settle it right.
Beerbohm, *Hosts and Guests* (1918)	That is the root of the mischief. He feels that it is more blessed, etc., and that he is conferring rather than accepting a favor. He does not adjust himself. He forgets his place. He leads the conversation. He tries genially to draw you out. He never comments on the goodness of the food or wine. He looks at his watch abruptly and says he must be off. He doesn't say he has had a delightful time.
Wodehouse, *A Damsel in Distress* (1919)	Animals care nothing about keeping up appearances. Observe Bertram the Bull when things are not going just as he could wish. He stamps. He snorts. He paws the ground. He throws back his head and bellows. He is upset, and he doesn't care who knows it. Instances could be readily multiplied.

Short sentences, and their combination with anaphora, have a similar use in accounts of action less tangible. They can put motion into a case that has none of a literal kind.

The manner in which the account opens, shows it to be traditionary. It begins abruptly. It is nobody that speaks. It is nobody that hears. It is addressed to nobody. It has neither first, second, nor third person. It has every criterion of being a tradition. It has no voucher.

Paine, *The Age of Reason* (1795)

The constitution will go down, sir (nautically speaking), in the degeneration of the human species in England, and its reduction into a mingled race of savages and pigmies.
That is my proposition. That is my prediction. That is the event of which I give you warning. I am now going to prove it, sir.

Dickens, *Threatening Letter to Thomas Hood from an Ancient Gentleman* (1844)

What is the change that has taken place since we separated last August? It is this. The League of Nations is alive. It is alive and in action. It is fighting for its life. Probably it is fighting for all our lives.

Churchill, speech in the House of Commons (1935)

Short sentences have another specialized application we ought to note: to make invective more pungent. Giving each of several claims its own sentence lends punch to them. The relevant contrast in this case tends to lie between the brevity of the sentences and the indignation of the speaker. Feeling can seem compressed when put into short sentences, as when put into short words.

And, as to the man, is Mr. Hastings a man against whom a charge of bribery is improbable? Why, he owns it. He is a professor of it. He reduces it into scheme and system. He glories in it. He turns it to merit, and declares it as the best way of supplying the exigencies of the company. Why therefore

Burke, speech in the impeachment of Warren Hastings (1788)

should it be held improbable? – But I cannot mention this proceeding without shame and horror.

Hazlitt, *On Vulgarity and Affectation* (1821)

There is no selection, truth, or delicacy in such a mode of proceeding. It is affecting ignorance, and making it a title to wisdom. It is a vapid assumption of superiority. It is exceeding impertinence. It is rank coxcombry. It is nothing in the world else. To condemn because the multitude admire is as essentially vulgar as to admire because they admire.

Wells, *The New Machiavelli* (1911)

Anyhow – having done that, you ought to have stood the consequences and thought of other people. You could have ended it at the first pause for reflection. You didn't. You blundered again. You kept on. You owed a certain secrecy to all of us! You didn't keep it. You were careless. You made things worse. This engagement and this publicity!

6. *Lincoln and the short sentence.* Lincoln's letters are wonderfully terse. Some of them consist only of short sentences, and not too many of them, with a notable absence of subordinate clauses. (Sometimes he was encouraged in his brevity by the use of the telegraph.) They show the force that can be gained by the use of spare constructions. Here are a few specimens.

Lincoln, letter to Henry Asbury (1858)

DEAR SIR: – Yours of the 13th was received some days ago. The fight must go on. The cause of civil liberty must not be surrendered at the end of one or even one hundred defeats. Douglas had the ingenuity to be supported in the late contest both as the best means to break down and to uphold the slave interest. No ingenuity can keep these antagonistic elements in harmony long. Another explosion will soon come.

Yours truly, A. LINCOLN.

My Dear Sir: – I expect the result of the election went hard with you. So it did with me, too, perhaps not quite so hard as you may have supposed. I have an abiding faith that we shall beat them in the long run. Step by step the objects of the leaders will become too plain for the people to stand them. I write merely to let you know that I am neither dead nor dying. Please give my respects to your good family, and all inquiring friends.

Yours as ever, A. Lincoln.

Lincoln, letter to Alexander Sympson (1858)

My Dear Sir: God help me! It is said I have offended you. Please tell me how.

Yours very truly, A. Lincoln

Lincoln, letter to Jacob Collamer (1861)

Born February 12, 1809, in Hardin County, Kentucky. Education, defective. Profession, a lawyer. Have been a captain of volunteers in Black Hawk war. Postmaster at a very small office. Four times a member of the Illinois Legislature and was a member of the lower house of Congress.

Yours, etc., A. Lincoln.

Lincoln, reply to request for autobiographical sketch (1858)

Chapter Eight
SENTENCE STRUCTURE

Think of every sentence as having a core of sense that usually consists of its subject and verb. A useful convention treats a sentence as branching to the right if it adds information after the subject and verb are given. The label is meant to be literal: if you imagine the entire sentence on one line, the elaboration would all be to the right of the verb. Here is a simple example of a sentence branching to the right:

Defoe, *Robinson Crusoe* (1719)

I was born in the year 1632, in the city of York, of a good family, though not of that country, my father being a foreigner of Bremen, who settled first at Hull....

The sentence feeds knowledge to the reader one piece at a time. It is easy to follow. You understand each part before being served another.

A sentence branches to the left if it gives the reader a lot of information before the key point arrives.

Churchill, London radio broadcast (1940)

Here in this strong City of Refuge which enshrines the title-deeds of human progress and is of deep consequence to Christian civilization; here, girt about by the seas and oceans where the Navy reigns; shielded from above by the prowess and devotion of our airmen – we await undismayed the impending assault.

The first 45 words are buildup. They describe conditions in which something is going to happen, or about which something is going to be said. After this wait, the point arrives. It, too, involves waiting.

Right-branching and left-branching sentences give the

reader a different experience. A right-branching sentence is less work. Little has to be remembered. A left-branching sentence takes more effort to follow. It asks the reader to keep in mind what is being said until the point arrives. In return, though, left-branching sentences can create a climax. The words at the beginning store up energy that is released at the end. They also involve the reader more fully by requiring an investment in the progress of the sentence. And of course they provide relief from sentences of the other type; the two kinds can set each other off like any other alternatives in prose. The types can also be combined. Some sentences branch to the left and then to the right.

The distinction between sentences that branch to the right and left overlaps with the distinction between sentences that are *loose* and *periodic*. A loose sentence adds content as it goes along, but can be stopped at various places along the way and still make sense. The example a moment ago from Defoe is loose as well as right-branching: a period could have been put at every place where a comma appears, and the sentence would be grammatically complete. A periodic sentence saves important information for the end. You have to read the whole thing to understand what it means, because the words needed to complete the thought, and to make the sentence work grammatically, don't arrive until late.

This chapter looks at some notable varieties of sentences that branch. The most basic right-branching sentences are too common and unremarkable to be worth illustrating, but some other patterns and extensions create interesting effects. In a sense these all can be considered ways of making a sentence a longer and more involved rhetorical adventure for the reader and writer.

1. *Modification and description to the right.* A sentence can easily branch right with lots of modifiers: phrases and words that say more about a subject or object already

stated. A simple case is the list of adjectives. The liveliest examples involve criticism or denunciation.

Burke, *Thoughts on French Affairs* (1791)	He is, of all men, if I am not ill-informed, the most turbulent, seditious, intriguing, bold, and desperate.
Grattan, speech in the House of Commons (1812)	You cannot do it; your good sense and your good feelings forbid it; the feelings of your countrymen forbid it; – it is an interdict, horrible, unnatural, impossible!
Hazlitt, *Sir Walter Scott* (1825)	The cells of his memory are vast, various, full even to bursting with life and motion; his speculative understanding is empty, flaccid, poor, and dead.
Twain, letter to J.H. Twichell (1905)	This lust has rotted these nations; it has made them hard, sordid, ungentle, dishonest, oppressive.

Though less common, adverbs rather than adjectives can be stacked in about the same way:

Trollope, *The Last Chronicle of Barset* (1867)	She would scold him – frightfully, loudly, scornfully, and worse than all, continually.

Such trains of modifiers can have a cumulative weight that is more than the sum of their parts. They produce a collective impression, like a drawing made up of many strokes that are then seen as a whole. The litany also can wear down the reader and discourage scrutiny of each word for accuracy.

The sentences just shown are right-branching and also loose. They usually could have been stopped earlier, because they end in a list that need not continue. But the result is similar, and branches as much to the right, if the adjectives lead to a thing modified that ends the clause. It is, again, an excellent device for vilification and grievance.

Grattan, speech in the Irish Parliament (1790)	Sir, the revenue laws are absurd, tyrannical, and contradictory; they are composed of little, capricious, spiteful, ignorant, unconstitutional, and interested clauses.

I love the pure, peaceable, and impartial Christianity of Christ; I therefore hate the corrupt, slave-holding, women-whipping, cradle-plundering, partial and hypocritical Christianity of this land.

Narrative of the Life of Frederick Douglass (1845)

He is a bewildered, confounded, and miserably perplexed man.

Lincoln, speech in the House of Representatives (1848)

I felt as if I had come from the clouds, where I had been leading a romantic life for ages, to a bawling, splashing, link-lighted, umbrella-struggling, hackney-coach-jostling, patten-clinking, muddy, miserable world.

Dickens, *David Copperfield* (1850)

You have not only the honor of being my steward, but the privilege of being the worst, most incompetent, drivelling snivelling jibbering jabbering idiot of a steward in France.

Shaw, *Saint Joan* (1923)

Those sentences branch to the right, but they aren't loose. The adjectives build toward a subject to which they apply. The endings thus produce a different payoff than we had in the first set of examples.

A related pattern strings together nouns, or short noun phrases, to achieve a similar effect. Instead of labeling a subject or object with an adjective or adverb, the items on the list restate or redescribe it.

I say, Sir, that, according to my conscientious conviction, we are now fixing on the Constitution of the United States, and its frame of government, a monstrosity, a disfiguration, an enormity!

Webster, speech in the Senate (1848)

Miserable distorted blockheads, the generality; ape-faces, imp-faces, angry dog-faces, heavy sullen ox-faces; degraded underfoot perverse creatures, sons of indocility, greedy mutinous darkness, and in one word, of STUPIDITY, which is the general mother of such.

Carlyle, *Model Prisons* (1850)

Shaw, *Man and Superman*
(1903)

Marriage is to me apostasy, profanation of the sanctuary of my soul, violation of my manhood, sale of my birthright, shameful surrender, ignominious capitulation, acceptance of defeat.

Or a right-branching list can be made of examples that describe different features of a subject.

Dickens, *Bleak House* (1853)

His family is nothing but bills, dirt, waste, noise, tumbles downstairs, confusion, and wretchedness.

Hawthorne, *English Notebooks*
(1856)

I think the poorer classes of Glasgow excel even those in Liverpool in the bad eminence of filth, uncombed and unwashed children, drunkenness, disorderly deportment, evil smell, and all that makes city poverty disgusting.

Twain, *The Innocents Abroad*
(1869)

Such was our daily life on board the ship – solemnity, decorum, dinner, dominoes, devotions, slander.

Mencken, *George Jean Nathan*
(1919)

Men so constantly associated with actors tend to take on the qualities of the actor – his idiotic vanity, his herculean stupidity, his chronic underrating of his betters.

2. *Elaboration to the right.* It is a short step from those examples to cases in which a sentence branches right for the sake of elaboration. The writer does not quite present a list, but rather enlarges and explains in successive phrases.

Henry, speech at Virginia
Ratifying Convention (1788)

Our legislature will indeed be a ludicrous spectacle – one hundred and eighty men marching in solemn, farcical procession, exhibiting a mournful proof of the lost liberty of their country, without the power of restoring it.

Cobden, speech in the House
of Commons (1854)

It will not do always to assume that the weaker party is in the right, for little States, like little individuals, are often very quarrelsome, presuming on their weakness, and not unfrequently abusing the forbearance which their weakness procures them.

They stood, as it were, in a living grave, dead to the events that stirred the globe's great populations, dead to the common interests of men, isolated and outcast from brotherhood with their kind.

Twain, *Roughing It* (1872)

I see advancing upon all this, in hideous onslaught, the Nazi war machine, with its clanking, heel-clicking, dandified Prussian officers, its crafty expert agents, fresh from the cowing and tying down of a dozen countries.

Churchill, London radio broadcast (1941)

All these cases start with a subject or object to be described – the legislature, little states, the war machine – and then add three or four phrases that elaborate on it. Notice that a period could have been put in place of most of the commas, but instead the description rolls on. This approach keeps the sentences easy to read despite their length, because the reader understands each bit perfectly before going on to the next. And if the end is convincing, what was noted along the way is easily accepted. It was scenery during the ride.

3. *Multiplied objects.* Extensions to the right can also arise by adding matter more substantial than modifiers and restatements. If the verb is transitive (that is, if it takes an object), one can apply it to a *series* of objects or complements.

The French had shown themselves the ablest architects of ruin that had hitherto existed in the world. In that very short space of time they had completely pulled down to the ground their monarchy, their church, their nobility, their law, their revenue, their army, their navy, their commerce, their arts, and their manufactures.

Burke, speech in the House of Commons (1790)

Macaulay, speech in the
House of Commons (1831)

Then would come agitation, tumult, political associations, libels, inflammatory harangues.

The list of objects or complements to set up a contrast with a shorter truth:

Shaw, *Major Barbara* (preface)
(1907)

The crying need of the nation is not for better morals, cheaper bread, temperance, liberty, culture, redemption of fallen sisters and erring brothers, nor the grace, love and fellowship of the Trinity, but simply for enough money. And the evil to be attacked is not sin, suffering, greed, priestcraft, kingcraft, demagogy, monopoly, ignorance, drink, war, pestilence, nor any other of the scapegoats which reformers sacrifice, but simply poverty.

4. *Multiplied verbs.* Extending sentences to the right with simple verbs or with participles can create a sense of onrush, activity, and compressed narrative.

Twain, *Roughing It* (1872)

Brown threw off his coat and challenged the man to fight – abused him, threatened him, impeached his courage, and urged and even implored him to fight.

This pattern was a favorite of Dickens.

Dickens, *Nicholas Nickleby*
(1839)

Never was man so tickled with a respectable old joke, as John Browdie was with this. He chuckled, roared, half suffocated himself by laughing large pieces of beef into his windpipe, roared again, persisted in eating at the same time, got red in the face and black in the forehead, coughed, cried, got better, went off again laughing inwardly, got worse, choked, had his back thumped, stamped about, frightened his wife, and at last recovered in a state of the last exhaustion and with the water streaming from his eyes, but still faintly ejaculating, "godfeyther – a godfeyther, Tilly!" in a tone bespeaking an exquisite relish of the sally, which no suffering could diminish.

He was mad for the moment; tearing out his hair, beating his head, trying to force me from him, and to force himself from me, not answering a word, not looking at or seeing anyone; blindly striving for he knew not what, his face all staring and distorted – a frightful spectacle.

Dickens, *David Copperfield* (1858)

Strings of verbs can create a feeling of activity that is endless, or at least tiresome.

Men fight and make up; repent and go at it; feast and starve; laugh and weep; pray and curse; cheat, chaffer, trick, truckle, cozen, defraud, fib, lie, beg, borrow, steal, hang, drown – as in the laughing and weeping, tricking and truckling, hanging and drowning times that have been.

Melville, *Mardi* (1849)

We are always appearing, and disappearing, and swearing, and interrogating, and filing, and cross-filing, and arguing, and sealing, and motioning, and referring, and reporting, and revolving about the Lord Chancellor and all his satellites, and equitably waltzing ourselves off to dusty death, about costs.

Dickens, *Bleak House* (1853)

5. *Independent clauses.* Sentences can branch to the right, of course, just by the use of conjunctions to join independent clauses – that is, by stitching together strings that could have stood as separate sentences if the writer had preferred. The use of this pattern to join two sentences is commonplace. The use of it to join three is less often seen, and so perhaps more interesting. It can produce a felt relationship between the elements – of causal connection, of forward motion, and sometimes of excitability in the speaker.

Would that he consumed his own smoke! for his smoke is horrible to inhale, and inhale it you must, and not only that, but you must live in it for the time.

Melville, *Moby-Dick* (1851)

Lincoln, Second Inaugural Address (1865)

Both parties deprecated war, but one of them would *make* war rather than let the nation survive, and the other would *accept* war rather than let it perish, and the war came.

Churchill, speech at Jerusalem (1921)

We think it is good for the world, good for the Jews, and good for the British Empire, and it is also good for the Arabs dwelling in Palestine, and we intend it to be so.

In the negative:

Emerson, *Spiritual Laws* (1841)

Over all things that are agreeable to his nature and genius the man has the highest right. Everywhere he may take what belongs to his spiritual estate, nor can he take any thing else though all doors were open, nor can all the force of men hinder him from taking so much.

6. *Narratives.* A final way to create a dramatic branching to the right: the narrative in which new phrases or clauses keep adding new rounds of action. Loading the elements into the same sentence, one after another, helps create a mural that the reader views with the writer's help.

Burke, *Reflections on the Revolution in France* (1790)

Their heads were stuck upon spears and led the procession, whilst the royal captives who followed in the train were slowly moved along, amidst the horrid yells, and shrilling screams, and frantic dances, and infamous contumelies, and all the unutterable abominations of the furies of hell in the abused shape of the vilest of women.

The narrative of the future:

Churchill, speech at Fulton, Missouri (1946)

Why cannot they share their tools and thus increase each other's working powers? Indeed they must do so or else the temple may not be built, or, being built, it may collapse, and we shall all be proved again unteachable and have to go and try to learn again for a third time in a school of war, incomparably more rigorous than that from which we have just been released.

The narrative can also be conceptual, as in this case from Shaw.

> Security, the chief pretense of civilization, cannot exist where the worst of dangers, the danger of poverty, hangs over everyone's head, and where the alleged protection of our persons from violence is only an accidental result of the existence of a police force whose real business is to force the poor man to see his children starve whilst idle people overfeed pet dogs with the money that might feed and clothe them.

Shaw, *Major Barbara* (preface) (1907)

7. *Left-branching subjects.* The left-branching sentence – especially when it amounts to a periodic construction (so that the sense of the sentence isn't complete until the end) – sounds less spontaneous than the right-branching or loose kind. The speaker seems to know from the start where the sentence is going to end. And these patterns also put more strain on the reader, who has to remember more as the sentence goes along. So nobody wants a heavily periodic style now, and left-branching patterns should be used with some care, but they still are useful in their place. This section and the next one show a few ways in which left-branching patterns can be put to work.

We started our look at right-branching patterns with lists that were tacked on after the core of a sentence. Patterns like that can also run to the left. A sentence may have more than one subject, or a subject (or object) with different aspects that can be recited before the verb arrives.

> Danger, enterprise, hope, the novel, the aleatory, are dearer to man than regular meals.

Stevenson, *The Day After Tomorrow* (1887)

Doyle, *How the Brigadier Triumphed in England* (1903)

Wine, women, dice, cards, racing – in all forms of debauchery he had earned for himself a terrible name.

In these cases the list gives the subject clarity or life by stating it in examples or with words that overlap. But that much could have been done by putting the list at the end of the sentence rather than the beginning. Putting it first primes the reader to receive the point by filling the mind with the relevant ideas.

A list of subjects also can help create a comprehensive quality: the speaker effectively means everything.

Burke, *Speech on American Taxation* (1774)

Your commerce, your policy, your promises, your reasons, your pretenses, your consistency, your inconsistency, – all jointly oblige you to this repeal.

Dickens, *David Copperfield* (1850)

Penitence, humiliation, shame, pride, love, and trustfulness – I see them all; and in them all, I see that horror of I don't know what.

Chesterton, *The Optimism of Byron* (1903)

Books, love, business, religion, alcohol, abstract truth, private emotion, money, simplicity, mysticism, hard work, a life close to nature, a life close to Belgrave Square are every one of them passionately maintained by somebody to be so good that they redeem the evil of an otherwise indefensible world.

The same approach can be used with subjects that aren't easily reduced to words on a list. Instead the subjects come in phrases.

Douglass, *My Bondage and My Freedom* (1855)

To tear off the mask from this abominable system, to expose it to the light of heaven, aye, to the heat of the sun, that it may burn and wither it out of existence, is my object in coming to this country.

Wilde, *The Decay of Lying* (1891)

The crude commercialism of America, its materializing spirit, its indifference to the poetical side of things, and its lack of imagination and of high

unattainable ideals, are entirely due to that country having adopted for its national hero a man who,
according to his own confession, was incapable of
telling a lie.

Restating the subject in these ways predisposes the
reader toward the mood the author wants when the
action arrives. The restatements at the start are sufficiently loaded to help win the argument before it starts.

A sentence can branch to the left in a similar manner
when the subject or object of the sentence is stated in an
involved phrase or series of them. The left branch consists of a long statement of a thing (not restatement) that
receives comment afterwards.

> But how hell should become by degree so natural,   Defoe, *Moll Flanders* (1722)
> and not only tolerable, but even agreeable, is a
> thing unintelligible but by those who have experi-
> enced it, as I have.

> What justice and uprightness there was in begin-   Paine, *The American Crisis*
> ning a war with America, the world will judge of,   (1783)
> and the unequalled barbarity with which it has
> been conducted, is not to be worn from the mem-
> ory by the cant of sniveling hypocrisy.

The left branches in those sentences creates interest by
posing a monetary question or mystery. With the reader's
curiosity raised, the sentence then comments on how it
might be satisfied. In more extreme cases, the substance
of the sentence lies mostly in the run-up to a minor
conclusion:

> As for such who read books only to find out the   Defoe, *An Essay Upon Projects*
> author's faux pas, who will quarrel at the mean-   (1697)
> ness of style, errors of pointing, dullness of expres-
> sion, or the like, I have but little to say to them.

Dickens, *Threatening Letter to Thomas Hood from An Ancient Gentleman* (1844)

What the condition of this country will be, when its standing army is composed of dwarfs, with here and there a wild man to throw its ranks into confusion, like the elephants employed in war in former times, I leave you to imagine, sir.

Putting the principal claims of a sentence into its preamble can be an effective rhetorical device. It treats their accuracy as a given; they are stated on the way to the main point. When we finish with the preamble and get to the formal action of the sentence ("I leave you to imagine"), we discover that the preamble *was* the point.

8. *Left-branching modifiers and conditions.* Another left-branching pattern starts with conditions that bear on the subject or under which the action occurs; then comes the action.

Paine, *The American Crisis* (1783)

Removed from the eye of that country that supports them, and distant from the government that employs them, they cut and carve for themselves, and there is none to call them to account.

Douglass, *My Bondage and My Freedom* (1855)

Conscious of the injustice and wrong they are every hour perpetrating, and knowing what they themselves would do if made the victims of such wrongs, they are looking out for the first signs of the dread retribution of justice.

Putting the conditions first creates an appetite in the reader for the point that follows. You can imagine rewriting these sentences to put the conditions after the subject and verb (with a "because," etc.) and see the difference. There would be no comparable climax. Stating background conditions in advance can also make the sense of the payoff follow with ease, as in these cases:

Lincoln, Second Inaugural Address (1865)

Now, at the expiration of four years, during which public declarations have been constantly called forth on every point and phase of the great contest which still absorbs the attention and engrosses the energies of the nation, little that is new could be presented.

But when you are as old as I am; when you have a thousand times wearied of heaven, like myself and the Commander, and a thousand times wearied of hell, as you are wearied now, you will no longer imagine that every swing from heaven to hell is an emancipation, every swing from hell to heaven an evolution.

Shaw, *Man and Superman* (1903)

The first part of Lincoln's sentence suggests activity and some exhaustion, so the arrival of his point at the end seems natural. Shaw's sentence works in a similar way. As we have seen, points in a preamble also tend to escape full scrutiny. If they came *after* the point they support, they would be more likely to invite challenge.

More extreme cases keep adding clauses in order to rile the audience or otherwise build anticipation. The hammer is theatrically raised and raised again before being brought down hard.

Show the thing you contend for to be reason, show it to be common sense, show it to be the means of attaining some useful end, and then I am content to allow it what dignity you please.

Burke, *Speech on American Taxation* (1774)

If the energy of man can compass the discovery of your fraud and treachery before your death; if wealth, revenge, and just hatred, can hunt and track you through your windings; you will yet be called to a dear account for this.

Dickens, *Nicholas Nickleby* (1839)

Therefore, when I saw so much nervous apprehension that, if I were permitted to speak – when I found they were afraid to have me speak – when I found that they considered my speaking damaging to their cause – when I found that they

Beecher, speech at Liverpool (1863)

appealed from facts and reasonings to mob law – I said, No man need tell me what the heart and secret counsel of these men are. They tremble and are afraid.

The hammer lowered with irony:

Churchill, speech in the House of Commons (1940)

If after all his boastings and bloodcurdling threats and lurid accounts trumpeted round the world of the damage he has inflicted, of the vast numbers of our Air Force he has shot down, so he says, with so little loss to himself; if after tales of the panic-stricken British crushed in their holes cursing the plutocratic Parliament which has led them to such a plight – if after all this his whole air onslaught were forced after a while tamely to peter out, the Fuhrer's reputation for veracity of statement might be seriously impugned.

Or the subject may be preceded or accompanied by words that paint it in detail before the arrival of the action.

Gibbon, *History of the Decline and Fall of the Roman Empire* (1776)

This famous monument, the authenticity of which many have attempted to impeach, rather from hatred to the Jesuits, by whom it was made known, than by a candid examination of its contents, is now generally considered above all suspicion.

Webster, speech at New York (1837)

He is a rash man indeed, and little conversant with human nature, and especially has he a very erroneous estimate of the character of the people of this country, who supposes that a feeling of this kind is to be trifled with or despised.

Dickens, *Little Dorrit* (1857)

Bending over a steaming vessel of tea, and looking through the steam, and breathing forth the steam, like a malignant Chinese enchantress engaged in the performance of unholy rites, Mr F.'s Aunt put down her great teacup and exclaimed, "Drat him, if he an't come back again!"

The same pattern, though the long run-up modifies an object:

> A spare, dark, withered man, of about his own age, with a stooping body, and a very sinister face rendered more ill-favoured by hollow and hungry cheeks, deeply sunburnt, and thick black eyebrows, blacker in contrast with the perfect whiteness of his hair; roughly clothed in shabby garments, of a strange and uncouth make; and having about him an indefinable manner of depression and degradation – this, for a moment, was all he saw.

Dickens, *Nicholas Nickleby* (1839)

9. *Branching both ways.* Sentences may, of course, branch to the left and *then* to the right. This can produce an attractive feeling of balance if the phrases on either side of the fulcrum are roughly even in extent.

> But his unbiased opinion, his mature judgment, his enlightened conscience, he ought not to sacrifice to you, to any man, or to any set of men living.

Burke, *Speech to the Bristol Electors* (1774)

> So violent an outrage upon credit, property, and liberty, as this compulsory paper currency, has seldom been exhibited by the alliance of bankruptcy and tyranny, at any time, or in any nation.

Burke, *Reflections on the Revolution in France* (1791)

Churchill used dual-branching sentences to produce graceful effects of that kind: a gentle walk up a hill, then back down.

> The gratitude of every home in our Island, in our Empire, and indeed throughout the world, except in the abodes of the guilty, goes out to the British airmen who, undaunted by odds, unwearied in their constant challenge and mortal danger, are turning the tide of the World War by their prowess and by their devotion.

Churchill, speech in the House of Commons (1940)

Churchill, speech in the
House of Commons (1940)

I have, myself, full confidence that if all do their duty, if nothing is neglected, and if the best arrangements are made, as they are being made, we shall prove ourselves once again able to defend our Island home, to ride out the storm of war, and to outlive the menace of tyranny, if necessary for years, if necessary alone.

Some slightly less balanced cases of branching both ways, which match the energy or unruliness that they mean to describe:

de Quincey, *Note Book of an English Opium Eater* (1855)

In the Pythian fury of his gestures – in his screaming voice – in his directness of purpose, Fox would now remind you of some demon steam-engine on a railroad, some Fire-king or Salmoneus, that had counterfeited, because he could not steal, Jove's thunderbolts.

Dickens, *A Tale of Two Cities* (1859)

Thus, with beer-drinking, pipe-smoking, song-roaring, and infinite caricaturing of woe, the disorderly procession went its way, recruiting at every step, and all the shops shutting up before it.

Right-branching and left-branching patterns can also be paired in separate consecutive sentences. The pattern is a kind of chiasmus: similar branching patterns appear at end of the first sentence and the start of the second.

Macaulay, *The History of England* (1855)

The majority of the House more justly regarded him as the falsest, the most malignant and the most impudent being that had ever disgraced the human form. The sight of that brazen forehead, the accents of that lying tongue, deprived them of all mastery over themselves.

Dickens, *A Tale of Two Cities* (1859)

Everything was bowed down, dejected, oppressed, and broken. Habitations, fences, domesticated animals, men, women, children, and the soil that bore them – all worn out.

Let us go forward together in all parts of the Empire, in all parts of the Island. There is not a week, nor a day, nor an hour to lose.

Churchill, speech at Manchester (1940)

Chapter Nine

THE PASSIVE VOICE

A passive clause is one in which the subject might be said to receive an action (or to be "acted upon") by the verb. Here is a rule of thumb for spotting passive clauses: a phrase identifying the doer of the act – "by him," "by her," "by them," or some comparable wording – appears after the verb or (more often) can be inserted silently without any grammatical problem.

An example: "All men are created equal." Is this active or passive? Passive: at the end you could add a "by" clause that names the party who did the creating ("…by God," or "by nature," or whatever else).

Another example: "These are the times that try men's souls." Active or passive? It's active. Some writers mistakenly call this sentence passive because it uses the word "are" (and so could be rewritten "These times try men's souls."). But the subject is not at the receiving end of any action, and there is no "by" clause that you could possibly add to complete the thought. A passive version of the sentence would be "Souls are tried by these times."

The passive voice suffers from an undeserved bad reputation. Some writers regard it as at least presumptively a vice. It isn't a vice at all. The passive is highly useful and is found often in good English writing. Most people are better off not worrying about it one way or the other. If a sentence is convoluted because it's passive, by all means make it active – not to avoid the passive voice, but to avoid being convoluted. Superstitious writers sometimes change passive to active just because a teacher once told them to, and their writing gets worse rather than better. The real problem is *thoughtless* use of the passive, or thoughtless avoidance of it.

The only rule really worth worrying about is simple: have a reason for whatever you do in your writing. That is how this chapter means to help. It shows some of the reasons (not all of them) why you might want to use the passive. The categories are informal, and some of the examples could reasonably appear in more than one of them.

1. *To subordinate the doer.* The speaker wants to focus on the recipient of an action rather than the doer of it, perhaps because the doer is of secondary interest or entirely beside the point. To go back to an example from a moment ago:

> We hold these truths to be self-evident, that all men are created equal, that they are endowed by their Creator with certain unalienable rights, that among these are life, liberty and the pursuit of happiness.

Declaration of Independence (1776)

If you want to say that God endows people with certain inalienable rights, you can phrase the point in two ways: it can be about God, or it can be about people. English allows for both:

> Their Creator endows all men with certain inalienable rights. (Active)

> All men are endowed by their Creator with certain inalienable rights. (Passive)

Jefferson's primary aim was to make a claim about people and their rights, not about their creator. So the creator is suppressed in one clause (*all men are created equal*) and subordinated in the other (*they are endowed by their Creator...*). In other words, he used the passive voice and was right to do so. Another such case:

> Never in the field of human conflict was so much owed by so many to so few.

Churchill, speech in the House of Commons (1940)

The action in the sentence is *owing*. The active form might be, "Never in the field of human conflict did so many owe so much to so few." That would have been fine English as well, but Churchill didn't want to put the recipients of the protection into such a position of emphasis. He preferred to emphasize what they owed, and to keep the few and the many next to each other. The passive version has a better rhythm, too.

In that case the passive voice keeps the emphasis where it belongs. The doer is named but given a subordinate position. As we've seen, you can press the emphasis further by leaving out the doer entirely.

Julius Cæsar, 3, 2

The evil that men do lives after them;
The good is oft interred with their bones.

Rewriting the second line to make it active – as by starting with who does the interring – would spoil it by giving undue emphasis to something irrelevant (never mind the meter). We don't care who does the interring. Here are some more cases where the doer of the act is of such lesser importance as to warrant omission.

Burke, *Speech on American Taxation* (1774)

Invention is exhausted; reason is fatigued; experience has given judgment; but obstinacy is not yet conquered.

Johnson, *Taxation No Tyranny* (1775)

When it is urged, that they will shoot up, like the hydra, he naturally considers how the hydra was destroyed.

Melville, *Moby-Dick* (1851)

"Damn him, cut!" roared Stubb; and so the whale was lost and Pip was saved.

2. *Multiple doers.* The passive voice is helpful when the action in a sentence has more than one doer. Putting all the doers first can leave the reader waiting a long time to find out what they did. The passive voice lets the author explain what the action was before (or without) naming everyone who contributed to it.

His guilt was fully established; and a party among the Whigs called loudly and importunately for his head. But he was saved by the pathetic entreaties of his brother Rochester, by the good offices of the humane and generous Burnet, and by Mary's respect for the memory of her mother.

Macaulay, *The History of England* (1855)

And all this evil is made possible by the schoolmaster with his cane and birch, by the parents getting rid as best they can of the nuisance of children making noise and mischief in the house, and by the denial to children of the elementary rights of human beings.

Shaw, *A Treatise on Parents and Children* (1910)

This really vital piece of vandalism was done by the educated, not the uneducated; it was done by the influence of the artists or antiquaries who wanted to preserve the antique beauty of Stonehenge.

Chesterton, *The Aristocratic 'Arry* (1912)

3. *To make the doers vague and numerous.* The passive voice can make a class of actors – most commonly the class of people who say or think something – seem large and amorphous.

And Crispin Crispian shall ne'er go by,
From this day to the ending of the world,
But we in it shall be remembered.

Henry V, 4, 3

It has been said that ingenious men may say ingenious things, and that those who are interested in raising the few upon the ruins of the many, may give to every cause an appearance of justice.

Hamilton, speech at New York Ratifying Convention (1788)

History has been ransacked to find examples of tyrants sufficiently odious to illustrate him by comparison. Language has been tortured to find epithets sufficiently strong to paint him in description.

Benton, speech in the Senate (1837) (on Andrew Jackson)

Lincoln, debate with Stephen Douglas at Peoria (1854)	Threats of the breaking up of the Union were freely made, and the ablest public men of the day became seriously alarmed.
Eliot, *Middlemarch* (1872)	He had travelled in his younger years, and was held in this part of the county to have contracted a too rambling habit of mind.

4. *The general or universal passive.* Suppressing the doer of an act can make a claim about it seem general or universal. The implied words at the end of the passive clause might be considered *by anyone* if that helps you see why the construction is passive. But in truth there really isn't any relevant doer. The speaker is making a claim about the world. Often it's a claim that something can't be done.

Carlyle, *Model Prisons* (1850)	Good from you, and your operations, is not to be expected.
Dickens, *Hard Times* (1854)	Teach these boys and girls nothing but Facts. Facts alone are wanted in life.
Lincoln, speech at Cooper Institute (1860)	Human action can be modified to some extent, but human nature cannot be changed.
Burke, *Reflections on the Revolution in France* (1790)	A king is not to be deposed by halves.

The passive voice can also make action appear to come from some stronger or more general source than the speaker's own self.

Hazlitt, *The Spirit of the Age* (1825)	A too restless display of talent, a too undisguised statement of all that can be said for and against a question, is perhaps the great fault that is to be attributed to him.
Lincoln, Second Inaugural Address (1865)	… as was said three thousand years ago, so still it must be said, "The judgments of the Lord are true and righteous altogether."

Again, you can (if you like) insert an imaginary "by" clause into these cases: "so still it must be said (by all of us)," maybe. It's artificial, but might help satisfy you that the clause is passive – if you care. But then why would you?

5. *Modesty and concealment.* Sometimes the passive voice is used, and the doer of an act suppressed entirely, when it nevertheless is clear enough who the doer is. The reasons vary. It may be a question of dignity or self-effacement.

> What the white whale was to Ahab, has been hinted; what, at times, he was to me, as yet remains unsaid.

Melville, *Moby-Dick* (1851)

> With high hope for the future, no prediction in regard to it is ventured.

Lincoln, Second Inaugural Address (1865)

The author is the actor, and the reader knows it. But the passive voice gets the speaker off the stage and throws all the attention onto what has been spoken (or not).

Speakers may also use the passive voice to suppress themselves for a different reason: to avoid responsibility, as when Macbeth considers whether to murder the king:

> If it were done when 'tis done, then 'twere well It were done quickly.

Macbeth, 1, 7

The passive voice, with the use of *it*, lets him think about the killing without thinking about his role. The assignment of responsibility may also be avoided because it isn't relevant:

> There may be mistakes made sometimes; and things may be done wrong, while the officers of the Government do all they can to prevent mistakes. But I beg of you, as citizens of this great Republic, not to let your minds be carried off from the great work we have before us.

Lincoln, Address to the 164th Ohio Regiment (1864)

6. *Emphasis at the end.* The passive voice can emphasize the doer of an act precisely by putting the doer *last*; for the end of a sentence is an emphatic placement. And apart from emphasis, the passive voice may create a more satisfying finish because it makes the end of the sentence, where the doer is named, climactic.

Burke, letter to William Elliott (1795)

Lincoln, letter to Henry Hoffman (1864)

Gibbon, *History of the Decline and Fall of the Roman Empire* (1776)

How often has public calamity been arrested on the very brink of ruin by the seasonable energy of a single man!

I attempt no argument. Argument upon the question is already exhausted by the abler, better informed, and more immediately interested sons of Maryland herself.

But all force may be annihilated by the negligence of the prince and the venality of his ministers.

That example from Lincoln also illustrates the use of the passive voice to create an echo of a particular word – in this case, "argument." Sometimes the passive allows an arrangement of words that is rhetorically appealing in some way of this kind.

Stevenson, *The Strange Case of Dr. Jekyll and Mr. Hyde* (1886)

Or, if you shall so prefer to choose, a new province of knowledge and new avenues to fame and power shall be laid open to you, here, in this room, upon the instant; and your sight shall be blasted by a prodigy to stagger the unbelief of Satan.

Churchill, speech in the House of Commons (1940)

May it not also be that the cause of civilization itself will be defended by the skill and devotion of a few thousand airmen?

7. *To emphasize the passivity of the recipient.* The passive voice fits well when the speaker wants to portray someone as the victim of a wrong, attack, or other such action. The victim is made to seem passive in the ordinary as well as the grammatical sense. The doers of the act aren't

necessarily suppressed or even subordinated; as we just saw, naming the doers at the end of a sentence can call more attention to them than an earlier mention would. It is a productive exercise to mentally rewrite these sentences in active form and ask what they lose.

O, I am spoil'd, undone by villains!

Othello, 5, 1

Oliver Cromwell's protectorate, or dictatorate, if you will let me name it so, lasted for about ten years, and you will find that nothing which was contrary to the laws of heaven was allowed to live by Oliver.

Carlyle, speech at the University of Edinburgh (1866)

The public has been practiced upon by writers who seem to find a kind of luxury in panic and alarm; and who endeavor to propagate these feelings throughout the country without success.

Gladstone, speech at Greenwich (1871)

Yesterday, December 7th, 1941 – a date which will live in infamy – the United States of America was suddenly and deliberately attacked by naval and air forces of the Empire of Japan.

Roosevelt, Message to Congress (1941)

Chapter Ten

ANACOLUTHON
AND RELATED DEVICES

Anacoluthon occurs when a writer changes the grammatical structure of a sentence in midstream. The device can create an impression of live, spontaneous thought being worked into language in front of the listener, and sometimes of feeling, confusion, or excitement that can't be contained by ordinary syntax. It stands out against the ordinary sentences that serve as its backdrop. (In return comes the occasional risk that the reader will think the author has made a blunder.)

In this chapter we consider as well some other minor devices that disrupt the usual flow of a sentence, whether by setting forth a subject and then stopping to comment on it, repeating a subject after taking a detour away from it, or in some other way.

1. *Grammatical or stylistic disruption*, in which the end of the sentence fails in some way to square with the expectations created beforehand. One might debate whether each of these next examples involves an outright grammatical stumble or just a stylistic one, as when parts that should be parallel aren't. The effect either way is the same: it's a bit jarring, and can convey a passion that doesn't have time for perfect order.

Emmet, statement at his trial for treason (1803)

I do not fear to approach the omnipotent Judge, to answer for the conduct of my whole life; and am I to be appalled and falsified by a mere remnant of mortality here? By you, too, who, if it were possible to collect all the innocent blood that you have shed in your unhallowed ministry, in one great reservoir, your lordship might swim in it.

Emmet wasn't thinking about sentence structure. He was thinking about being hanged. The point is just that the grammatical disruption in the last sentence isn't a flaw. It's an advantage. Sometimes a careful writer allows such disruptions; they can also convey a casual and natural sensibility, and a lack of interest of being too tidy in the expression of a point.

> There were likewise two ensigns, both very young fellows; one of whom had been bred under an attorney, and the other was son to the wife of a nobleman's butler.

Fielding, *Tom Jones* (1749)

> As for the Pyramids, there is nothing to wonder at in them so much as the fact that so many men could be found degraded enough to spend their lives constructing a tomb for some ambitious booby, whom it would have been wiser and manlier to have drowned in the Nile, and then given his body to the dogs.

Thoreau, *Walden* (1854)

2. *Reconsideration,* in which the author veers away from a sentence to say something different. Sometimes this amounts to a kind of *aposiopesis* (speech that breaks off). But here the speaker stops more to change direction than to leave things unsaid. It is an interruption of oneself. Thoughts compete for expression.

> O, Mr. Booth, it is a cruel reflection! and could I after this have expected from you – but why not from you, to whom I am a person entirely indifferent, if such a friend could treat me so barbarously?

Fielding, *Amelia* (1751)

> When my eyes were opened to his real character – Oh! had I known what I ought, what I dared to do! But I knew not – I was afraid of doing too much. Wretched, wretched mistake!

Austen, *Pride and Prejudice* (1813)

> You might copy out and post the specially-provided letter without making yourself ridiculous in the

Beerbohm, *How Shall I Word It?* (1920)

eyes of its receiver – unless, of course, he or she also possessed a copy of the book. But – well, can you conceive any one copying out and posting one of these letters, or even taking it as the basis for composition? You cannot.

3. *The restarted sentence*. Here the author sets out a short phrase or clause, then restarts the sentence in order to comment on what has been set forth or to ask a question about it. The separation gives the reader a moment to breathe. It also throws a certain emphasis onto whatever came before the break. The simplest pattern of this kind states a subject and then talks about it.

de Quincey, *The Household Wreck* (1838)

That night – that first night of separation from my wife – how it passed, I know not; I know only that it passed.

Lincoln, speech at Indianapolis (1861)

The people – when they rise in mass in behalf of the Union and the liberties of their country, truly may it be said, "The gates of hell cannot prevail against them."

The speaker thus calls attention to the subject by setting it off from the rest of the sentence, as if the topic were put on a table and then examined. Sometimes the subject, having been presented in this way, is made the focus of a question.

Coleridge, *Table Talk* (1833)

All the Greek writers after Demosthenes and his contemporaries, what are they but the leavings of tyranny, in which a few precious things seem sheltered by the mass of rubbish!

Thoreau, *On the Duty of Civil Disobedience* (1849)

This American government – what is it but a tradition, though a recent one, endeavoring to transmit itself unimpaired to posterity, but each instant losing some of its integrity?

Melville, *Moby-Dick* (1851)

When that wicked king was slain, the dogs, did they not lick his blood?

A ruffian on a horse – what is there that he will
not ride over, and ride on, careless and proud of
his own shame?

Kingsley, *The Ancien Regime* (1867)

The restart after a list:

Penitence, humiliation, shame, pride, love, and
trustfulness – I see them all; and in them all, I see
that horror of I don't know what.

Dickens, *David Copperfield* (1850)

Army, Navy, Air Force, religion, law, language, culture, institutions, literature, history, tradition – all
are to be effaced by the brute strength of trium-
phant Army and the scientific low cunning of a
ruthless police force.

Churchill, London radio broadcast (1940)

Gesturing back to the subject with a word of recapitula-
tion (*this* or *these* in the examples below) can add another
layer of emphasis. When the run-up to the verb gets long,
such a word also helps the reader manage the length of
what has already been said.

That all this should be said by the very men who
bid us search the Scriptures, and call themselves
the servants and the delegates of a crucified God –
this, I do honestly confess, provokes indignation;
makes one stamp the foot, and cry out "monstrous" at every word!

Sheil, undated speech

This pattern lends itself well to condemnation. A word
like "this" then points back at what was just said with
disappointment or censure.

The registry club, the reading-room, the polling
booths – these are the only positions in the country we can occupy. Voters' certificates, books, pamphlets, newspapers – these are the only weapons
we can employ.

Meagher, speech at Dublin (1846)

What a man's name was, what his income was,
whom he married, where he lived, these are not
sanctities; they are irrelevancies.

Chesterton, *Charlotte Brontë* (1903)

Churchill, London radio
broadcast (1943)

Nazi tyranny and Prussian militarism, which threatened to engulf the whole world, and against which we stood alone for a fateful year – these curses will have been swept from the face of the earth.

4. *Resumption with repetition.* These constructions restart a sentence partway through, but this time the new start repeats one already made. The repetition brings attention to the subject and refreshes the recollection. Simple examples:

Boswell (to Johnson), *Life of Johnson* (1791)

But, Sir, does not affecting a warmth when you have no warmth, and appearing to be clearly of one opinion when you are in reality of another opinion, does not such dissimulation impair one's honesty?

Corwin, speech in the Senate
(1847)

I dare say, when Tamerlane descended from his throne built of seventy thousand human skulls, and marched his ferocious battalions to further slaughter, I dare say he said, "I want room."

Douglass, speech at Rochester
(1850)

The moment a foreigner ventures upon our soil, and utters a natural repugnance to oppression, that moment he is made to feel that there is little sympathy in this land for him.

In longer cases the language of resumption again helps the listener manage the length of the claim.

Dickens, *David Copperfield*
(1850)

It is not for one situated, through his original errors and a fortuitous combination of unpropitious events, as is the foundered Bark (if he may be allowed to assume so maritime a denomination), who now takes up the pen to address you – it is not, I repeat, for one so circumstanced, to adopt the language of compliment, or of congratulation.

I can only account for his having done so upon the supposition that that evil genius which has attended him through his life, giving to him an apparent astonishing prosperity, such as to lead very many good men to doubt there being any advantage in virtue over vice, – I say I can only account for it on the supposition that that evil genius has at last made up its mind to forsake him.

Lincoln, debate with Stephen Douglas at Freeport (1858)

Churchill made much use of this pattern.

The terrible military machine which we and the rest of the civilized world so foolishly, so supinely, so insensately allowed the Nazi gangsters to build up year by year from almost nothing – this machine cannot stand idle, lest it rust or fall to pieces.

Churchill, London radio broadcast (1941)

I do not grudge our loyal, brave people, who were ready to do their duty no matter what the cost, who never flinched under the strain of last week – I do not grudge them the natural, spontaneous outburst of joy and relief when they learned that the hard ordeal would no longer be required of them at the moment; but they should know the truth.

Churchill, speech in the House of Commons (1938)

Anything more foolish than to suppose that the life and strength of the Royal Navy – which, allow me to remind the House, is engaged in bringing in through the U-boats the immense traffics of this country – anything, I say, more foolish than to suppose that the life and strength of the Royal Navy should have been expended in ceaselessly patrolling up and down the Norwegian and Danish coasts, a target for the U-boats, wearing out their crews and machinery on the chance that Hitler would launch a blow like this – anything more foolish than that nobody can imagine.

Churchill, speech in the House of Commons (1940)

The same idea, but with resumption after *parenthetical* language (with or without parentheses):

Campbell-Bannerman, speech at London (1905)

What lesson, then, are we to draw – for let us always be taught by the conduct of our enemies – what lesson are we to draw from their discomfiture?

Churchill, London radio broadcast (1940)

Behind these soldiers of the regular Army, as a means of destruction for parachutists, air-borne invaders, and any traitors that may be found in our midst (but I do not believe there are many – woe betide them, they will get short shrift) – behind the regular Army we have more than a million of the Local Defense Volunteers, or, as they are much better called, the "Home Guard."

5. *Parentheticals and asides.* As just shown, parentheticals let the author exit the flow of a sentence for a moment. They can be uninteresting in the common case where they just mention some point that is minor. But sometimes they permit other effects, such as letting the writer draw closer to the members of the audience by talking to them more directly.

Fielding, *Tom Jones* (1749)

As Molly pronounced those last words, which are recorded above, the wicked rug got loose from its fastening, and discovered everything hid behind it; where among other female utensils appeared – (with shame I write it, and with sorrow will it be read) – the philosopher Square, in a posture (for the place would not near admit his standing upright) as ridiculous as can possibly be conceived.

Eliot, *Middlemarch* (1872)

Mr. Casaubon was touched with an unknown delight (what man would not have been?) at this childlike unrestrained ardor: he was not surprised (what lover would have been?) that he should be the object of it.

But (it seems that I must begin every paragraph by questioning the sincerity of what I have just said) has the gift of laughter been withdrawn from me?

Beerbohm, *Laughter* (1920)

These parentheticals create a separate track of commentary that is more intimate than the main line.

Parentheticals also let points be made in an undertone. Sometimes the undertone is fitting because what is said is sharper or rougher than the rest of the sentence; a parenthetical is a good place for the poke or put-down. It sequesters those kinds of remarks from the rest of the discourse, and so treats them as subordinate while also calling a different kind of attention to them.

This rage for raising goods is for several reasons much more the fault of the Tories than the Whigs; and yet the Tories (to their shame and confusion ought they to be told of it) are by far the most noisy and discontented.

Paine, *The American Crisis* (1783)

It has been the misfortune (not, as these gentlemen think it, the glory) of this age, that everything is to be discussed, as if the Constitution of our country were to be always a subject rather of altercation than enjoyment. For this reason, as well as for the satisfaction of those among you (if any such you have among you) who may wish to profit of examples, I venture to trouble you with a few thoughts upon each of these establishments.

Burke, *Reflections on the Revolution in France* (1790)

Ten or twelve years ago, being engaged in a bombastic discussion with what was then known as an intellectual Socialist (like the rest of the intelligentsia, he succumbed to the first fife-corps of the war, pulled down the red flag, damned Marx as a German spy, and began whooping for Elihu Root, Otto Kahn and Abraham Lincoln), I was greatly

Mencken, *Professor Veblen* (1919)

belabored and incommoded by his long quotations from a certain Prof. Dr. Thorstein Veblen, then quite unknown to me.

As seen a moment ago, comments parenthetical in spirit need not be enclosed in parentheses. Dashes can do the job, or (in spoken cases) just a turning aside from the normal flow of the sentence to offer a jab.

Mencken, *The Late Mr. Wells* (1919)

The prophesying business is like writing fugues; it is fatal to every one save the man of absolute genius. The lesser fellow – and Wells, for all his cleverness, is surely one of the lesser fellows – is bound to come to grief at it, and one of the first signs of his coming to grief is the drying up of his sense of humor.

Or compare these two examples:

Burke, *Reflections on the Revolution in France* (1790)

Abstractedly speaking, government, as well as liberty, is good; yet could I, in common sense, ten years ago, have felicitated France on her enjoyment of a government (for she then had a government) without inquiry what the nature of that government was, or how it was administered?

Churchill, speech at Harvard University (1943)

The great Bismarck – for there were once great men in Germany – is said to have observed towards the close of his life that the most potent factor in human society at the end of the nineteenth century was the fact that the British and American peoples spoke the same language.

6. *False endings and fragments.* An exclamation point or question mark can appear in the thick of a sentence without finishing it. This device helps to suggest excitability; the fever of the writer is too much for ordinary punctuation. It can also help toward engagement with the audience, as if the speaker is in a dialogue. This first example is from a speech, so its punctuation is perhaps

conjectural, but it suggests the idea as it might arise in spontaneous form.

> This armament, delayed until any man of common sense must have seen its total inutility towards its professed object, arrives at Genoa, just in time – for what? to assist General Melas? No, – but just in time to have the earliest intelligence of his total ruin.

Fox, speech in the House of Commons (1801)

A written example of the same pattern that seeks the feel of live speech:

> The steward advances, and with a benevolent, consolatory glance hands him – what? Some hot Cognac? No! hands him, ye gods! hands him a cup of tepid ginger and water!

Melville, *Moby-Dick* (1851)

A largely lost classical pattern drops an exclamatory fragment into a sentence to convey animation or fury. This, too, can aid a feeling of engagement. A side outburst is made to the listener or reader.

> You know they are fighting and dying in your service, and in this knowledge you learn the falsehood of the calumnies which were once offered against their pretensions; and what is more, oh shame to relate it! admitted as evidence; their opponents said that no Irish Catholic could be loyal to a prince of the House of Hanover.

Grattan, speech in Parliament (1812)

> I was kept for some time in the French Exhibition Room, and thought I should not be able to get a sight of the old masters. I just caught a peep at them through the door (vile hindrance!) like looking out of purgatory into paradise.

Hazlitt, *On the Pleasures of Painting* (1825)

> She was always, I seem to remember, fetching me; fetching me for a meal, fetching me for a walk or, detestable absurdity! fetching me for a wash and

Wells, *The New Machiavelli* (1911)

brush up, and she never seemed to understand anything whatever of the political systems across which she came to me.

Runs of such fragments can raise indignation to a high pitch.

Grattan, speech in the Irish Parliament (1788)

They said, that those who paid not their tithes, would be found guilty before God; and if they did not give the tenth, that God would reduce the country to a tenth. Blasphemous preachers! gross ignorance of the nature of things! impudent familiarity with the ways of God! audacious, assumed knowledge of his judgments, and a false denunciation of his vengeance!

Grattan, speech in the Irish Parliament (1790)

Sir, that corruption should be practiced by ministers is a common case; that it should be carried under the present administration to that most extraordinary and alarming excess, is the peculiar misfortune of the country, and the peculiar disgrace of her government, in their present venal hands. But that this should be justified! That this should be justified in Parliament! Corruption expressly justified in Parliament!

Webster, speech in the Senate (1850)

To break up this great government! to dismember this glorious country! to astonish Europe with an act of folly such as Europe for two centuries has never beheld in any government or any people! No, sir! no, sir! There will be no secession!

A specialized use of exclamatory fragments: the incredulous repetition of another's claims.

Emmet, statement at his trial for treason (1803)

I am charged with being an emissary of France! An emissary of France!

Webster, Reply to Hayne (1830)

Has he disproved a fact, refuted a proposition, weakened an argument, maintained by me? Has he come within beat of drum of any position of mine? O, no; but he has "carried the war into the enemy's country"! Carried the war into the enemy's country!

Sir, I have no patience with this flagitious notion of fighting for indemnity, and this under the equally absurd and hypocritical pretense of securing an honorable peace. An honorable peace!

Corwin, speech in the Senate (1847)

Serial cases:

But, Sir, the Coalition! The Coalition! Ay, "the murdered Coalition!" The gentleman asks, if I were led or frighted into this debate by the specter of the Coalition. "Was it the ghost of the murdered Coalition," he exclaims, "which haunted the member from Massachusetts; and which, like the ghost of Banquo, would never down?" "The murdered Coalition!"

Webster, Reply to Hayne (1830)

But the Secretary for the Treasury exclaims, "If the agitators would but let us alone, and allow Ireland to be tranquil." The agitators, forsooth! Does he venture – has he the intrepidity to speak thus? Agitators!

Sheil, speech in the House of Commons (1834)

What! no capital! Is my mastery of Greek no capital? Is my access to the subtlest thought, the loftiest poetry yet attained by humanity, no capital? my character! my intellect! My life! my career! what Barbara calls my soul! are these no capital?

Shaw, *Major Barbara* (1907)

But see:

"Oh, Louisa!" cried Miss Tox. "How can you speak to me like that?" "How can I speak to you like that?" retorted Mrs. Chick, who, in default of having any particular argument to sustain herself upon, relied principally on such repetitions for her most withering effects.

Dickens, *Dombey and Son* (1848)

Chapter Eleven

THE RHETORICAL INSTRUCTION

This chapter considers devices in which the speaker tells or asks the listener to do something: to observe, to imagine, to try an experiment. These methods, too, can produce involvement; the reader or listener is called on to participate. Some of the classic patterns for this purpose are a little archaic now, but we'll look at them anyway. It is good to see how these things have been done.

These may be considered part of a family of rhetorical techniques that vary the author's relationship to the audience and close the distance between them. Usually the writer or speaker stands in a consistent posture toward the reader or listener. The detachment between them, whatever its extent, stays about the same; the writer typically doesn't call attention to their relationship but just says what there is to be said. The instruction and other forms of direct address provide relief from that pattern.

1. *Recommended experiments.* Inviting the audience to try something enlists them in the speaker's project. They are asked not just to listen but to picture, not just to sit but to engage in activity, even if imagined. The speaker then helps with a description, or prediction, of the result.

Henry, speech at Virginia Ratifying Convention (1788)	Look for an example of a voluntary relinquishment of power, from one end of the globe to another: you will find none.
Burke, *Reflections on the Revolution in France* (1790)	Trace them through all their artifices, frauds, and violences, you can find nothing at all that is new.
Lincoln, letter to Samuel Galloway (1859)	Try a thousand years for a sound reason why Congress shall not hinder the people of Kansas from

having slaves, and, when you have found it, it will be an equally good one why Congress should not hinder the people of Georgia from importing slaves from Africa.

Multiplying the experiments:

Repeal the Missouri Compromise, repeal all com-promises, repeal the Declaration of Indepen-dence, repeal all past history, you still cannot repeal human nature.

Lincoln, debate with Stephen Douglas at Peoria (1854)

In reality, there is, perhaps, no one of our natural passions so hard to subdue as pride. Disguise it, struggle with it, beat it down, stifle it, mortify it as much as one pleases, it is still alive, and will every now and then peep out and show itself.

Autobiography of Benjamin Franklin (1791)

Here, take what standard you will, the result will be the same. Take population: take the rental: take the number of ten pound houses: take the amount of the assessed taxes: take any test in short: take any number of tests, and combine those tests in any of the ingenious ways which men of science have suggested: multiply: divide: subtract: add: try squares or cubes: try square roots or cube roots: you will never be able to find a pretext for excluding these districts from Schedule C.

Macaulay, speech in the House of Commons (1832)

Constructions with *go* involve the listeners by inviting their participation in imagined travels.

Go where you may, search where you will, roam through all the monarchies and despotisms of the old world, travel through South America, search out every abuse, and when you have found the last, lay your facts by the side of the every-day practices of this nation, and you will say with me, that, for revolting barbarity and shameless hypoc-risy, America reigns without a rival.

Douglass, speech at Rochester (1852)

Gladstone, speech in the
House of Commons (1886)

Go into the length and breadth of the world, ran-
sack the literature of all countries, find, if you can,
a single voice, a single book, find, I would almost
say, as much as a single newspaper article, unless
the product of the day, in which the conduct of
England towards Ireland is anywhere treated
except with profound and bitter condemnation.

Time travel:

Lincoln, debate with Stephen
Douglas at Alton (1858)

Go back to the day of the Missouri Compromise.
Go back to the nullification question, at the bottom of which lay this same slavery question. Go
back to the time of the annexation of Texas. Go
back to the troubles that led to the Compromise
of 1850. You will find that every time, with the
single exception of the Nullification question,
they sprung from an endeavor to spread this
institution.

Constructions with *let* can set forth conditions that prepare the stage for the arrival of a conclusion. Most of
these cases could be written with if/then phrasing; this
would cause no loss of meaning but some loss of engagement with the audience, which no longer is invited
to help.

Madison, Federalist 46 (1787)

Let a regular army, fully equal to the resources of
the country, be formed; and let it be entirely at the
devotion of the federal government; still it would
not be going too far to say, that the State governments, with the people on their side, would be
able to repel the danger.

Melville, *Moby-Dick* (1851)

Let the most absent-minded of men be plunged
in his deepest reveries – stand that man on his
legs, set his feet a-going, and he will infallibly lead
you to water, if water there be in all that region.

Sometimes an experiment can be recommended without comment on what will come of it. These constructions are similar to rhetorical questions: the result is self-evident.

> But tread on the toe of one of these amiable and imperturbable mortals, or let a lump of soot fall down the chimney and spoil their dinners, and see how they will bear it.

Hazlitt, *Lord Eldon and Mr. Wilberforce* (1825)

> If you think you can slander a woman into loving you or a man into voting for you, try it till you are satisfied!

Lincoln, speech at New Haven (1860)

2. *Instructions to look and see.* Another device for interacting with the audience: not an experiment, but directions to the mind's eye.

> I then said that I feared that the next war which should be kindled in Europe would be a war not so much of armies as of opinions. Not four years have elapsed, and behold my apprehension realized!

Canning, speech in the House of Commons (1826)

> Behold the practical operation of this internal slave trade – the American slave trade sustained by American politics and American religion! Here you will see men and women reared like swine for the market.

Douglass, speech at Rochester (1852)

> The deed was not then accomplished, neither did he confide in me. Observe! Under those circumstances even, I do not offer my testimony.

Dickens, *A Tale of Two Cities* (1859)

> And now as to the original conspirators, what has become of them? Some of them are dead; and as to those who are still living, I ask you, sir, are they not dead also? Look at Jefferson Davis himself.

Schurz, speech in the Senate (1872)

Directions of this kind can be multiplied in the same way as the experiments seen earlier.

Grattan, speech in the Irish
Parliament (1787)

This is not the first time I have had occasion to express my concern at certain excesses of some part of our fellow-subjects. See the fruit of those excesses! see the glorious effect of their labour! a riot act aggravated! a riot act general and perpetual! Evils which it was chance to foresee, it becomes now my duty to mitigate.

Constructions with *here* and *there* allow the speaker to gesture again with pointed finger, and so to direct the imagination to a real or figurative point and its significance.

Webster, argument in the trial
of John Francis Knapp (1830)

The club was found near the spot, in a place provided for it, in a place that had been previously hunted out, in a concerted place of concealment. *Here was their point of rendezvous.* Here might the lights be seen. Here might an aid be secreted. Here was he within call. Here might he be aroused by the sound of the whistle. Here might he carry the weapon. Here might he receive the murderer after the murder.

Melville, *Moby-Dick* (1851)

And for years afterwards, perhaps, ships shun the place; leaping over it as silly sheep leap over a vacuum, because their leader originally leaped there when a stick was held. There's your law of precedents; there's your utility of traditions; there's the story of your obstinate survival of old beliefs never bottomed on the earth, and now not even hovering in the air! There's orthodoxy!

Churchill, speech in the
House of Commons (1939)

Now, there is the breach; there is the violation of the pledge; there is the abandonment of the Balfour Declaration; there is the end of the vision, of the hope, of the dream.

Extended applications can call the attention of the audience to imaginary but specific sights and sounds. (In classical jargon, these probably are best considered cases of *hypotyposis*.)

Follow this drove to New Orleans. Attend the auction; see men examined like horses; see the forms of women rudely and brutally exposed to the shocking gaze of American slave-buyers. See this drove sold and separated forever; and never forget the deep, sad sobs that arose from that scattered multitude. Tell me, citizens, where, under the sun, can you witness a spectacle more fiendish and shocking.

Douglass, speech at Rochester (1852)

Listen! No, listen carefully; I think I hear something – yes, there it is quite clear. Don't you hear it? It is the tramp of armies crunching the gravel of the parade-grounds, splashing through rain soaked fields, the tramp of two million German soldiers and more than a million Italians – "going on maneuvers" – yes, only on maneuvers! Of course it's only maneuvers – just like last year.

Churchill, London radio broadcast (1939)

Melville favored this technique.

But now forget all about blinds and whiskers for a moment, and, standing in the Right Whale's mouth, look around you afresh. Seeing all these colonnades of bone so methodically ranged about, would you not think you were inside of the great Haarlem organ, and gazing upon its thousand pipes?

Melville, *Moby-Dick* (1851)

Not one in fifty of the actual disasters and deaths by casualties in the fishery, ever finds a public record at home, however transient and immediately forgotten that record. Do you suppose that that poor fellow there, who this moment perhaps caught by the whale-line off the coast of New Guinea, is being carried down to the bottom of the sea by the sounding leviathan – do you suppose that that poor fellow's name will appear in the newspaper obituary you will read to-morrow at your breakfast?

Melville, *Moby-Dick* (1851)

3. *The command or wish*. Now some more aggressive applications of these patterns, as when the author suspends exposition to implore or command the audience.

Samuel Adams, speech at
Philadelphia (1776)

Let us not be so amused with words! the extension of her commerce was her object.

Hamilton, Fedcralist 11 (1788)

Disunion will add another victim to his triumphs. Let Americans disdain to be the instruments of European greatness!

James, *Pragmatism* (1907)

The conditioned ways in which we do think are so much irrelevance and matter for psychology. Down with psychology, up with logic, in all this question!

Away with constructions have been made a good device for dramatic instruction in the thick of argument.

Hamilton, Camillus 18 (1795)

Away with these absurd and incongruous sophisms! Blush, ye apostles of temerity, of meanness, and of deception!

Grattan, speech in the Irish
Parliament (1782)

Away with doubtful construction and inexplicit security! We are enslaved, unless we are freed by an English act of parliament! Away with the charters of Ireland, and the distinct inherent rights of the land: let us have the English Parliament expressly legalize the independency of the Parliament of Ireland; establish the liberty of Ireland by virtue of an English act! Away with the flimsy bubble, security of a covenant between nation and nation: let us bind the Parliament of England by its laws!

A less forensic application:

Beerbohm, *On Speaking
French* (1919)

But heaven protect us from the foreigner who pauses, searches, fumbles, revises, comes to standstills, has recourse to dumb-show! Away with him, by the first train to Dover!

As that last case suggests, exclamations of these kinds can also step away from direct exposition to express the passionately felt wish or prayer.

> But may the just vengeance of the people overtake the authors of these pernicious counsels! May the loss of the first province of the empire be speedily followed by the loss of the heads of those ministers who have persisted in these wicked, these fatal, these most disastrous measures!

Wilkes, speech in Parliament (1775)

> To be sure, no prognosticating symptoms of these things have as yet appeared, – nothing even resembling their beginnings. May they never appear! May these prognostications of the author be justly laughed at and speedily forgotten!

Burke, letter to the Earl Fitzwilliam (1795)

4. *Challenge and defiance.* We turn, finally, to confrontational interactions with the audience, as when the speaker asks for a showing.

> Show me that age and country where the rights and liberties of the people were placed on the sole chance of their rulers being good men, without a consequent loss of liberty!

Henry, speech at Virginia Ratifying Convention (1788)

> If any man will produce the Koran to me, and will but show me one text in it that authorizes in any degree an arbitrary power in the government, I will confess that I have read that book, and been conversant in the affairs of Asia, in vain.

Burke, speech in the impeachment of Warren Hastings (1788)

> I deny that the public ever demanded any such thing – ever repudiated the Missouri Compromise, ever commanded its repeal. I deny it, and call for the proof.

Lincoln, debate with Stephen Douglas at Peoria (1854)

The challenge or defiance can be personal rather than conceptual.

Grattan, speech in Parliament (1790)

We pronounce them to be public criminals! Will they dare to deny the charge? I call upon, and dare the ostensible member to rise in his place, and say on his honor that he does not believe such corrupt agreements have taken place. I wait for a specific answer.

Grattan, speech in Parliament (1800)

I have returned to refute a libel, as false as it is malicious, given to the public under the appellation of a Report of a Committee of the Lords. Here I stand ready for impeachment or trial. I dare accusation. I defy the honorable gentleman. I defy the Government; I defy their whole phalanx. Let them come forth.

Cobbett, *Remarks on the Pamphlets Lately Published Against Peter Porcupine* (1796)

I will, therefore, never write another word in reply to any thing that is published about myself. Bark away, hell-hounds, till you are suffocated in your own foam.

Chapter Twelve
THE RHETORICAL ANNOUNCEMENT

Here we look briefly at some final ways in which speakers can set off statements for emphasis. These generally involve signals that a claim of note is coming. The signal may be partly for the convenience of the audience, as it provides a short pause before driving forward. Or the signal may create emphasis by putting a frame around what follows. These are minor devices but worthwhile to observe because they do not follow from ordinary advice on style. Most of the sentences shown here could be made a little shorter without a loss of substance.

Some of the examples to come are also cases of anacoluthon; some are merely mild disruptions of the usual norms in expository writing or speech. Instead of just churning ahead, the writing becomes conscious of itself. The audience sees the speaker not only speaking, but speaking about speaking and directing the listener's attention.

1. *Words as colons.* Some arrangements of wording can operate like colons. They direct the focus of the audience. Constructions with *this*:

He that knows anything, knows this, in the first place, that he need not seek long for instances of his ignorance.

Locke, *An Essay Concerning Human Understanding* (1690)

Shakespeare and Scott are certainly alike in this, that they could both, if literature had failed, have earned a living as professional demagogues.

Chesterton, *Twelve Types* (1903)

As concerns tobacco, there are many superstitions. And the chiefest is this – that there is a *standard* governing the matter, whereas there is nothing of the kind.

Twain, *What is Man?* (1906)

Some more involved applications, with the signaling word moved back a bit:

Swift, *Thoughts on Various Subjects* (1706)

When a true genius appears in the world, you may know him by this sign, that the dunces are all in confederacy against him.

Johnson, *Cheynel* (1751)

There is always this advantage in contending with illustrious adversaries, that the combatant is equally immortalized by conquest or defeat.

Disraeli, speech on the Corn Laws (1841)

But this I will tell the right hon. Gentleman, that though he may not feel humiliated, his country ought to feel humiliated.

Churchill, speech in the House of Commons (1940)

Of this I am quite sure, that if we open a quarrel between the past and the present, we shall find that we have lost the future.

I mean.

Henry, speech at Virginia Ratifying Convention (1788)

But there is one thing in it which I never would acquiesce in. I mean, the changing it into a consolidated government, which is so abhorrent to my mind.

Cobden, speech at Rochdale (1859)

I have found in America that everywhere the question of education lies at the foundation of every political question. I mean this: that in America the influential classes, as you may call them, the richer people, everywhere advocate education for the people, as a means of enabling the people to govern themselves.

Constructions with *here*.

Shaw, *Back to Methuselah* (1921)

But meanwhile – and here comes the horror of it – our technical instruction is honest and efficient.

Borrow, *Lavengro* (1851)

Oh, how rejoiced was I with the present which had been made me, my joy lasted for at least five minutes; I would let them breed, I would have a

house of hawks; yes, that I would – but – and here
came the unpleasant idea – suppose they were to
fly away, how very annoying!

Constructions with *is*.

Every hour you continue on this ill-chosen ground, your difficulties thicken on you; and therefore my conclusion is, remove from a bad position as quickly as you can.	Burke, *Speech on American Taxation* (1774)
My guiding star always is, Get hold of portable property.	Dickens, *Great Expectations* (1861)
To these questions one answer only can be truly given, and that is, Force, in the widest sense of the word, must decide the question.	Stephen, *Liberty, Equality, Fraternity* (1873)

2. *Stating that one is making a statement.* A frame placed
around a sentence to call attention to it.

"What is this, my lord?" said one of those who surrounded him. "Have blows passed?" "*One* blow has," was the panting reply. "I struck him. I proclaim it to all here! I struck him, and he knows why."	Dickens, *Nicholas Nickleby* (1839)
It is a dreadful thing to say that Mr. W. B. Yeats does not understand fairyland. But I do say it.	Chesterton, *Orthodoxy* (1908)
And I say in the face of the world, I say in the face of those connected with, or likely to be benefited by, the Buffalo Convention, – I say to all of them, that there has been no party of men in this country which has firmly and sternly resisted the progress of the slave power but the Whigs.	Webster, speech at Marshfield (1848)

Grattan made fine use of this device.

There is no objection to this resolution, except fears; I have examined your fears, I pronounce them to be frivolous.	Grattan, speech in the Irish Parliament (1780)

Grattan, speech in the Irish Parliament (1783)	Such has been your conduct, and at such conduct every order of your fellow-subjects have a right to exclaim! The Merchant may say to you – the constitutionalist may say to you – the American may say to you – and I, I now say, and say to your beard, Sir, – you are not an honest man.
Grattan, speech in the Irish Parliament (1790)	Gentlemen talk of the protection afforded by the police. I will tell you to whom it is a protection, and to whom it is not; it is a protection to the obnoxious member of Parliament; it is a protection to him who has not innocence to protect himself; it is a place army for corrupt men. I will tell you to whom it is not a protection; it is not a protection to the citizen; it is not a protection to him who has not servants to protect himself against the robber.

The frame can indicate the spirit in which one's own statement is made.

Dickens, *Little Dorrit* (1857)	"Mr Clennam," she composedly interrupted, "recollect that I do not speak by implication about the man. He is, I say again without disguise, a low mercenary wretch."
Chesterton, *The Angry Author* (1912)	Therefore I repeat, with the wail of imprecation, don't say that the variety of creeds prevents you from accepting any creed. It is an unintelligent remark.

3. *Questions*. The same methods can set up a question.

Thackeray, *Vanity Fair* (1848)	How dare you, sir, mention that person's name before Miss Swartz to-day, in my drawing-room? I ask you, sir, how dare you do it?
Borrow, *The Romany Rye* (1857)	For the third time I ask you, O young man of Horncastle! why does your Government always send fools to represent it at Vienna?

Still, while for the world's good I refuse to further the cause of these mineral doctors, I would fain regard them, not as willful wrong-doers, but good Samaritans erring. And is this – I put it to you, sir – is this the view of an arrogant rival and pretender?

Melville, *The Confidence-Man* (1857)

And again the frame can explain the conditions or spirit of the question.

Now, I ask you in all soberness if all these things, if indulged in, if ratified, if confirmed and indorsed, if taught to our children, and repeated to them, do not tend to rub out the sentiment of liberty in the country, and to transform this government into a government of some other form.

Lincoln, speech at Chicago (1858)

But when I came to reckon up what remained to me of my capital, I found it amounted to something less than four hundred pounds! I ask you fairly – can a man who respects himself fall in love on four hundred pounds?

Stevenson, *New Arabian Nights* (1882)

I will avail myself of the avuncular relationship which I hope I may still possess in respect of the Government to put it to the Prime Minister personally and even intimately, Has he ever heard of Saint Anthony the Hermit? Saint Anthony the Hermit was much condemned by the fathers of the church because he refused to do right when the devil told him to.

Churchill, speech in the House of Commons (1938)

Chapter Thirteen

CADENCE: CLASSIC PATTERNS

This last part of the book examines another form of contrast, and in some ways the simplest of all: variation
between stressed and unstressed syllables. Such variation
is one aspect of the cadence of a sentence – that is, the
rhythmic flow between different sorts of sounds.
Cadence is a subtle matter that nevertheless can do much
to distinguish appealing prose from the rest. When a sentence strikes deep, it sometimes is hard to say just why.
The effect will probably have been produced by several
elements, none of which may be conscious for the writer
or reader. Cadence is one of them, and is worth more
attention than it tends to receive. Trollope made the
point in the following way, after discussing how one
learns to hear the difference between good and bad
poetry through long familiarity:

Trollope, *Autobiography* (1883)

And so will the writer become familiar with what
is harmonious in prose. But in order that familiarity may serve him in his business, he must so train
his ear that he shall be able to weigh the rhythm
of every word as it falls from his pen. This, when it
has been done for a time, even for a short time,
will become so habitual to him that he will have
appreciated the metrical duration of every syllable
before it shall have dared to show itself upon
paper. The art of the orator is the same. He knows
beforehand how each sound which he is about to
utter will affect the force of his climax. If a writer
will do so he will charm his readers, though his
readers will probably not know how they have
been charmed.

Our particular interest lies in the way that sentences, or distinct parts of them, *end*. The rhythms that occur before a pause are the most noticeable to the ear. Starting at the end of a sentence also gives us a clear point of analytical departure. Working backward from there, we can identify patterns that lead up to it without too many disputes about how to carve the rhythms up into feet or other units. Once the ear is sensitive to the rhythms that end sentences, the sensitivity can be transferred to other points; endings can be a workspace for thinking about rhythms throughout a sentence.

The hard part when writing about prose rhythm is reaching agreement about where the stresses go. I'll try to stick with examples where that's clear enough, but inevitably the reader won't agree about some of them. When rhythms of these kinds do seem distinct in prose, they usually arise from two principles. First, words of more than one syllable always have a primary accent on one syllable or another; that syllable takes stress. Second, significant words in a sentence – usually nouns and verbs, along with important modifiers – usually are stressed at the expense of articles, prepositions, and other small words. This is not a matter of rule, so in some cases I will be suggesting how a line is best read, not how it must be read.

This chapter will look at seven patterns for the arrangement of stress at the end of a sentence. There are many interesting patterns besides these seven, of course, but that will be more than enough for most readers. Studying rhythm in this way may seem artificial in any event. First, of course, the rhythm of prose should never become too regular and thus risk sounding like verse. (Quintilian said in *The Orator's Education* that "the occurrence of an entire verse in prose is more disgusting than anything, but even a part of a verse is disfiguring.") Second, nobody writes prose by trying to match the cadence of it with a pattern, and nobody should. If you fuss excessively, the likely result is too studied a sound. The realistic goal is just to listen when writing a sentence and consider whether slight rearrangement would produce a better rhythm. Yet it's useful to study principles systematically even if they have to be used unsystematically. The patterns are valuable to study and then to forget.

Talking about rhythm requires some sort of notation. I will follow the custom of referring to a stressed syllable with a slash and an unstressed syllable with an x. This sentence, for example –

de Quincey, *Note Book of an English Opium Eater* (1855)

Friends are as dangerous as enemies.

– would be described: / x x / x x x / x x (**friends** are as **dang**erous as **en**emies). I also will take the liberty of referring to a sequence like that as -2-3-2, where the hyphens refer to stressed syllables and the numbers refer to the number of unstressed syllables between the stressed ones. This discussion won't bother about lesser degrees of stress. We will crudely treat syllables as stressed or not, and for the sake of clarity I will also suggest the stressed ones with boldface.

1. *The iambic finish.*
x / x / x /
1–1–1–

If one unstressed syllable lies between each of the last three stressed ones in a sentence – in other words, if the pattern goes da DUM da DUM da DUM – the pattern is iambic. An "iamb" (*eye*-am) is a two-syllable unit in which the first syllable is weak and the second is strong. The iambic rhythm is common in English and easily engages the ear. It sometimes is called rising rhythm because each unit starts weak and ends strong, creating a sense of lift. This line from the King James Bible is usually considered an example (though of course there are other ways it *could* be read):

She **gave** me **of** the **tree** and **I** did **eat.**   Gen. 3:12

Some sentences with iambic endings that are more clear cut:

> Thereby he is driven to entertain himself alone   Emerson, *Compensation* (1841)
> and acquire habits of self-help; and thus, like the
> wounded oyster, he **mends** his **shell** with **pearl.**

> Savage men stood naked on the strand, and bran-   Melville, *Mardi* (1849)
> dished uncouth clubs, and **gnashed** their **teeth**
> like **boars.**

> Truth, Sir, is a cow which will yield such people no   Johnson, in Boswell's *Life*
> more milk, and so they are **gone** to **milk** the **bull.**   (1791)

> Every one of them is wondering which will be the   Churchill, London radio
> next victim on whom the criminal adventurers of   broadcast (1940)
> Berlin will **cast** their **rend**ing **stroke.**

A little longer:

> I'm not sure he was really meant by nature to be   James, *The Ambassadors* (1903)
> quite so good. It's like the new edition of an old
> book that one has been fond of – revised and
> amended, brought up to date, but not **quite** the
> **thing** one **knew** and **loved.**

> He cuts his way through life as if no one had ever   Woolf, *Thoreau* (1917)
> taken that road before, leaving these signs for
> those who come after, should they **care** to **see**
> which **way** he **went.**

The up-and-down quality of the iambic rhythm can make it a way to underscore repetitive wording.

> It was like the last feeble echo of a sound made   Dickens, *A Tale of Two Cities*
> **long** and **long** ago.   (1859)

> This frightful business is now unfolding **day** by   Churchill, London radio
> **day** be**fore** our **eyes.**   broadcast (1941)

The rhythms in those last two examples could be interpreted as *trochaic* (see below) rather than iambic – that is, as DA-dum rather than da-DUM. It's a matter of interpretation. But either way the rhythm is alternating and repetitive.

Long runs of iambs are common in verse, of course; five such feet in a row are called iambic pentameter. Shakespeare's plays consist mostly of lines like that. Once you know the iambic form when you hear it, you will run across long outbreaks of it from time to time. These probably are examples, though one might quibble over the emphasis of a syllable here and there:

Dickens, *The Mystery of Edwin Drood* (1870)

> There has been rain this afternoon, and a wintry shudder goes among the little pools on the cracked, uneven flag-stones, and **through** the **giant elm**-trees **as** they **shed** a **gust** of **tears.**

Melville, *Mardi* (1849)

> … like **Xerxes' brittle chains** which **vainly sought** to **bind** the **Helle**spont.

The last syllable of that final example might be read as unstressed, and as a break from the pattern.

2. *The trochaic finish.*

/ × / × / ×

–I–I–I

Stressed syllables can be alternated in a different way, moving from strong to weak instead of weak to strong. Rather than iambs, we are dealing then with *trochees* (pronounced *trow*-keez) – units of two syllables in which the first is stressed and the second unstressed, creating a pattern that in poetry would be called trochaic.

Ps. 34:13

> **Keep** thy **tongue** from **evil,** and thy **lips** from **speaking guile.**

Guile technically is a word of one syllable, but it ends with an unaccented sound.

Subdue your appetites, my dears, and you've con-quered **hu**man **na**ture.	Dickens, *Nicholas Nickleby* (1839)
All very fine, Mary; but my old-fashioned common sense is better than your **clever modern non**sense.	Shaw, *Love Among the Artists* (1900)

Trochees create what in verse is called falling rhythm, as opposed to the rising rhythm achieved when the pattern runs the other way. Sometimes falling rhythm works like a minor key in music to support a critical or somber assessment.

One fact, however, was striking, and fell in with the impression of his natural tiger character, that his face wore at all times a **blood**less **ghast**ly **pal**lor.	de Quincey, *Note Book of an English Opium Eater* (1855)
… moping about in a drizzling rain and looking as droopy and woebegone as so **ma**ny **molt**ing **chick**ens.	Twain, *The Innocents Abroad* (1869)

The falling rhythm of the trochaic pattern, along with the hammering quality produced by its repetitive character, also makes it especially fine for denunciation, tirade, and other sorts of oratorical aggression.

This is in itself most gross; but **con**trast **makes** it **mon**strous.	Sheil, speech in the House of Commons (1835)
That inscrutable thing is chiefly what I hate; and be the white whale agent, or be the white whale principal, I will **wreak** that **hate** up**on** him.	Melville, *Moby-Dick* (1851)
Sir, are they not words of **brill**iant **pol**ished **trea**son?	Baker, speech in the Senate (1861)

Some longer cases:

Thus are blown away the **in**sect **race** of **court**ly **false**hoods!	Burke, *Speech on American Taxation* (1774)
I should suffer the misery of devils, were I to make a whore of my soul by swearing allegiance to one	Paine, *The American Crisis* (1783)

whose character is that of a **sott**ish, **stu**pid, **stub**-born, **worth**less, **brut**ish man.

A cautionary note:

de Quincey, *Protestantism* (1847)

I should have described him more briefly as a "master-builder," had my ear been able to endure a sentence ending with two consecutive trochees, and each of those trochees ending with the same syllable *er*.

3. *The anapestic finish.*

/ × × / × × /

−2−2−

The balanced or symmetrical rhythm is an attractive pattern in prose. One good example involves three stressed syllables with two weak ones between each of them: a −2−2− sequence. The slow and even movement can create the sound of sober assessment, and of the truth. (Two weak syllables followed by a stress are known as an *anapest*, so this rhythm might be called anapestic – but it starts with a stress, too.)

Matt. 5:5

Blessed are the meek: for **they** shall in**her**it the **earth**.

Burke, *Thoughts on the Present Discontents* (1770)

If they refuse to give this proof, we **know** of what **stuff** they are **made**.

Webster, speech at Plymouth (1820)

If the pulpit be silent whenever or wherever there may be a sinner bloody with this guilt within the hearing of its voice, the **pul**pit is **false** to its **trust**.

James, *The Middle Years* (1909)

Our doubt is our passion and our passion is our task. The **rest** is the **mad**ness of **art**.

Churchill, London radio broadcast (1943)

These curses will have been **swept** from the **face** of the **earth**.

The motion of this rhythm can also make it good for describing action or even violence.

How long will ye vex my soul, and **break** me in **pie**ces with **words**?

Job 19:2

There shall be **wail**ing and **gnash**ing of **teeth**.

Matt. 13:42

The reluctant Basil suspended the treaty, accepted the defiance, and led his army into the land of heresy, which he **wast**ed with fire and **sword**.

Gibbon, *History of the Decline and Fall of the Roman Empire* (1776)

Exclamatory examples:

We are told, by that paper, that a regular statement and account of the receipts and expenditures of all public money shall be published from time to time. **Here** is a **beau**tiful **check**!

Henry, speech at Virginia Ratifying Convention (1788)

Those books, both prose and verse, are consecrated to me by other associations; and I hate to have them de**based** and pro**faned** in his **mouth**!

Brontë, *Wuthering Heights* (1847)

Never **dream** with thy **hand** on the **helm**!

Melville, *Moby-Dick* (1851)

These might be read as longer cases of the pattern:

To the one we are the **sa**vour of **death** unto **death**; and to the **oth**er the **sa**vour of **life** unto **life**.

2 Cor. 2:15

... shielded from above by the prowess and devotion of our airmen, we a**wait** undis**mayed** the im**pend**ing as**sault**.

Churchill, London radio broadcast (1940)

4. *The dactylic finish.*
/ × × / × × / × ×
–2 –2 –2

The sentences just seen ended with a stress. A balanced rhythm also can finish with a weak syllable at the end. A *dactyl* is a stressed syllable followed by two unstressed ones, so we can call this pattern dactylic.

Ps. 92:12	The righteous shall flourish like the palm-tree: he shall **grow** like a **ce**dar in **Leb**anon.
Burke, *Letter to a Noble Lord* (1796)	They have tigers to fall upon animated strength. They have hy**en**as to **prey** upon **car**casses.
Grattan, speech in Parliament (1808)	If they form a distinct society, they will be a distinct people, and will reap the **wag**es of **pride** and in**firm**ity.
James, *Washington Square* (1881)	He will **nev**er be **van**quished by **ar**gument.
Churchill, speech in the House of Commons (1944)	The Allied Forces, with the Americans in the van, are driving ahead, northwards, in re**lent**less pur**suit** of the **en**emy.
Lincoln, speech at Republican State Convention (1856)	And **well** may he **cling** to that **prin**ciple!

The pattern used twice:

Burke, *Reflections on the Revolution in France* (1790)	**Kings** will be **ty**rants from **pol**icy, when **sub**jects are **reb**els from **prin**ciple.

By letting the sentence trail off, the weak ending can lend itself well to expressions of resignation, despair, and disgust.

Defoe, *Robinson Crusoe* (1719)	I am cast upon a horrible, desolate island, **void** of all **hope** of re**cov**ery.
Grattan, speech in the Irish Parliament (1792)	…some of you went forth like a giant rejoicing in his strength; and now you stand like elves, at the **door** of your **own** pande**mon**ium.
Douglass, *My Bondage and My Freedom* (1855)	I will continue to pray, labor, and wait, believing that she cannot always be insensible to the dictates of justice, or **deaf** to the **voice** of hu**man**ity.

5. *Two dactyls, one trochee.*

/ × × / × × / ×

−2−2−1

Suppose we subtract one syllable from the end of that last pattern. It then becomes -2-2-1 (two dactyls and a trochee):

Yea, for thy sake are we killed all the day long; we are **coun**ted as **sheep** for the **slaugh**ter.

Ps. 44:22

This pattern is one of the great English cadences. It is prominent in the King James Bible. It conditions the ear to expect two weak beats between the strong ones, but just one arrives at the end; trimming back the rhythm in this way gives the finish a gently conclusive sound, as though the finish were neatly tucked in.

... a time to embrace, and a **time** to re**frain** from em**bra**cing.

Eccl. 3:5

... for **this** is the **law** and the **proph**ets.

Matt. 7:12

As the Biblical examples show, the balance of this rhythm lends itself well to advice, aphorism, or other sonorous statement.

Time makes more **con**verts than **rea**son.

Paine, *Common Sense* (1776)

Fear is an instructor of great sagacity and the **her**ald of **all** revolutions.

Emerson, *Compensation* (1841)

With unrelaxed nerves, with morning vigor, sail by it, looking another way, **tied** to the **mast** like Ulysses.

Thoreau, *Walden* (1854)

You say that you think slavery is wrong, but you de**nounce** all at**tempts** to re**strain** it.

Lincoln, speech at New Haven (1860)

The yoke a man creates for himself by wrong-doing will breed **hate** in the **kind**liest **na**ture.

Eliot, *Silas Marner* (1861)

Surely, here was something to ponder over, as a step in education; something that **tend**ed to **stag**ger a **scep**tic!

The Education of Henry Adams (1918)

Churchillian applications:

Churchill, *The Story of the Malakand Field Force* (1898)

Nature will **not** be ad**mi**red by **proxy**.

In the depths of that dusty soul is **noth**ing but **ab**ject sur**ren**der.

Churchill, quoted in Dalton, *Memoirs* (1957) (on Neville Chamberlain)

Churchill, speech to the
United States Congress (1952)

The sooner, also, will our sense of security, and the fact of our security, be seen to reside in valiant, resolute and well-armed manhood, rather than in the awful secrets which **science** has **wrest**ed from **nat**ure.

The pattern may be extended with more dactyls. The longer the example goes, the more room for dispute about it, but perhaps these are likely enough:

Gen. 3:2

And that woman said unto the serpent, We may **eat** of the **fruit** of the **trees** of the **gar**den.

Luke 15:13

And not many days after the younger son gathered all together, and took his journey into a far country, and there **was**ted his **sub**stance with **riot**ous **liv**ing.

Emerson, letter to Carlyle
(1871)

I hope the ruin of no young man's soul will here or hereafter be charged to me as having **wast**ed his **time** or con**found**ed his **rea**son.

Churchill, speech at
Birmingham (1909)

There is one feature in the guidance of the House of Lords by Lord Lansdowne which should specially be noticed, and that is the air of solemn humbug with which this ex-Whig is **al**ways at **pains** to in**vest** its pro**ceed**ings.

6. *One dactyl, two trochees.*

/ × × / × / ×

−2 −1 −1

Another combination.

Ex. 27:22

The voice is Jacob's voice, but the **hands** are the **hands** of Esau.

The effect is mild acceleration. The earlier distance between the stresses creates an open, looser sense. The quicker alternations resolve it, and tie a knot.

The poem of creation is uninterrupted; but **few** are the **ears** that **hear** it.

Thoreau, *Walden* (1854)

They hold together like bees; offend one, and **all** will re**venge** his **quar**rel.

Kingsley, *Westward Ho!* (1855)

Let us therefore brace ourselves to our duties, and so bear ourselves that, if the British Empire and its Commonwealth last for a thousand years, men will still say, "**This** was their **fin**est **hour**."

Churchill, speech in the House of Commons (1940)

7. *The spondaic finish.*
//

Stressed syllables don't always alternate with unstressed, so we might note some cases in which sentences end with two stressed syllables in a row (that is, with a *spondee*). It's a pattern that can create a decisive and emphatic finish.

Ye that dare oppose, not only the tyranny, but the tyrant, **stand forth**!

Paine, *Common Sense* (1776)

A fly, Sir, may sting a stately horse and make him wince; but one is but an insect, and the other is a **horse still**.

Johnson, in Boswell's *Life* (1791)

Circumstances are infinite, are infinitely combined; are variable and transient; he who does not take them into consideration is not erroneous, but **stark mad**.

Burke, *Speech on the Petition of the Unitarians* (1792)

Both parties deprecated war, but one of them would *make* war rather than let the nation survive, and the other would *accept* war rather than let it perish, and the **war came**.

Lincoln, Second Inaugural Address (1865)

Chapter Fourteen

CADENCE: COMBINATIONS
AND CONTRASTS

The previous chapter looked at some individual rhythms that can give a satisfying finish to a sentence or clause. Now we consider the results produced when different rhythmic ideas are combined in a sentence or in a pair of them. The difference that will interest us here is basic: it is movement between an ending with a stressed syllable and an ending with an unstressed one, or vice versa. Whatever the pattern that leads up to them, those ways of ending a sentence or clause sound different, and the different sounds can be played off against each other in attractive ways.

1. *Movement from weak to strong endings.* We begin with some sentences that use two rhythms. The first part of the sentence ends with an unstressed syllable (we might call this a soft or weak ending). The second part ends with a stressed syllable: a hard or strong ending. The earlier rhythm creates a tentative sound, or a lifting of the hammer; the strong finish brings the hammer down or creates a sense of completion. This is a frequent pattern in the King James Bible.

Gal. 6:7 | For whatsoever a man soweth, that shall he also reap.

Prov. 16:18 | Pride goeth before destruction, and an haughty spirit before a fall.

Matt. 13:25 | Every kingdom divided against itself is brought to desolation; and every city or house divided against itself shall not stand.

As those examples show, a classic use of this construction also employs the rhetorical device known as isocolon: clauses that are similar in length and parallel in structure.

> Render therefore unto Cæsar the things which are Cæsar's; and unto God the things that are God's.

Matt. 22:21

This sentence gains its lasting beauty in part from the repeated structure of the clauses and the words within them. But the rhythm also adds to the success of its sound: the upswing at the end of the first part, and the stressed monosyllable at the end of the second.

The impact can be enhanced by putting together two or three phrases with weak endings before ending with the strong one.

> When I was a child, I spake as a child, I understood as a child, I thought as a child: but when I became a man, I put away childish things.

1 Cor. 13:11

> If ye love wealth better than liberty, the tranquility of servitude than the animating contest of freedom – go from us in peace.

Samuel Adams, speech at Philadelphia (1776)

> They may be mistaken – they may be blinded by strong emotions – but corrupt they cannot be.

Sheil, argument for the defense in the trial of John O'Connell (1843)

The same idea can be used with a series of short items, too. The stressed ending of the last entry then gives it an extra dash of emphasis, and tells the ear that the sequence is done.

> Such a spirit is Liberty. At times she takes the form of a hateful reptile. She grovels, she hisses, she stings.

Macaulay, *Milton* (1825)

> In war, Resolution. In defeat, Defiance. In victory, Magnanimity. In peace, Goodwill.

Churchill, *The Second World War* (1948)

We have seen many examples of our theme combined with isocolon, or parallel structure. This rhythmic pattern also makes a handsome complement to a case of chiasmus, or reversed structure. Ending the first part with an unstressed syllable, and the last part with a stress, helps complete the closed loop.

Johnson, in Boswell's *Life* (1791)	It appears to me, that Huggins has ball without powder, and Warton powder without ball.
Lincoln, letter to A.G. Hodges (1864)	I claim not to have controlled events, but confess plainly that events have controlled me.
Chesterton, *Thoughts Around Koepenick* (1915)	In short, we do not get good laws to restrain bad people. We get good people to restrain bad laws.
Churchill, speech in the House of Commons (1943)	We shape our buildings, and afterwards our buildings shape us.

2. *Sound and sense.* Contrasting rhythms – here, a weak ending followed by a strong one – can help make the sound of a sentence drive home its meaning. In these cases, for example, the weight of the concluding stress underscores an ending in the substance:

Paine, *Letters to American Citizens* (1802) (on John Adams)	It has been the political career of this man to begin with hypocrisy, proceed with arrogance, and finish in contempt.
Grattan, speech in the Irish Parliament (1800)	I will remain anchored here – with fidelity to the fortunes of my country, faithful to her freedom, faithful to her fall.
Grattan, speech in the House of Commons (1805)	The Parliament of Ireland – of that assembly I have a parental recollection. I sat by her cradle, I followed her hearse.

Or the decisive stress at the finish can support the statement of a resolution or result.

Paine, *The American Crisis* (1783)	The nearer any disease approaches to a crisis, the nearer it is to a cure.

The louder he talked of his honor, the faster we counted our spoons.

Emerson, *Worship* (1860)

That last example also shows how a firm ending can puncture pretension. Notice that the first half of the sentence ends in fashion that is Latinate as well as unstressed. The climax is Saxon as well as stressed. That is a useful pairing: a fancy word with a weak ending at the end of the first clause, then a stressed and simple word at the end of the second. The last word has been set up to ring, burn, or produce a laugh.

The gentleman asks, When were the colonies emancipated? I desire to know, when were they made slaves?

Pitt, speech in the House of Commons (1766)

He has no enemies, but is intensely disliked by his friends.

attributed to Oscar Wilde

The rest is vanity; the rest is crime.

Burke, *Letters on a Regicide Peace* (1796)

Or consider, finally, the alignment of sound and sense in the endings shown here:

Opinion, I admit, will operate against opinion. But, as the honorable member for Kilkenny has observed, force must be used against force.

Meagher, speech at Dublin (1846)

When danger is far off we may think of our weakness; when it is near we must not forget our strength.

Churchill, speech at London (1939)

Our hands may be active, but our consciences are at rest.

Churchill, speech in the House of Commons (1939)

In the first two of those examples, discussion of weakness ends with weakness; discussion of strength ends with strength. In the last one, the weight of the stressed ending matches the conscience at rest.

3. *Movement from strong to weak endings.* Now the reverse of the pattern just shown: the stress comes at the end of

the first sentence (or the first half of the same sentence), and the second part ends without stress. The effect tends to be an unfurling quality. The strong ending early in the sentence creates a tightness or energy that is released by the soft ending of the last part.

Matt. 6:12	And forgive us our debts, as we forgive our debtors.
1 Cor. 15:55	O death, where is thy sting? O grave, where is thy victory?
Lincoln, speech at Springfield (1858)	I do not expect the Union to be *dissolved* – I do not expect the house to *fall* – but I *do* expect it will cease to be divided.
Burke, speech in the impeachment of Warren Hastings (1788)	An event has happened, upon which it is difficult to speak, and impossible to be silent.

As that last example from Lincoln shows, the pattern can be amplified by starting with multiple rounds of rhythms with strong endings, creating a bigger buildup that is let out in the soft finish.

Rev. 13:1	And I stood upon the sand of the sea, and saw a beast rise up out of the sea, having seven heads and ten horns, and upon his horns ten crowns, and upon his heads the name of blasphemy.
Fielding, *Tom Jones* (1749)	The captain made his advances in form, the citadel was defended in form, and at length, in proper form, surrendered at discretion.
Kingsley, *Superstition* (1867)	They must sting like wasps, revenge like wasps, hold altogether like wasps, build like wasps, work hard like wasps, rob like wasps; then, like the wasps, they will be the terror of all around, and kill and eat all their enemies.

And as that last instance from Kingsley shows, the effect is also furthered if earlier segments are notably shorter than the last one. The longer finish adds to the sense of compression released. Some more examples of the same:

> Have ye not known? have ye not heard? hath it not been told you from the beginning?
>
> Isa. 40:21

> For a Khan of the plank, and a king of the sea, and a great Lord of Leviathans was Ahab.
>
> Melville, *Moby-Dick* (1851)

> These are my fears, and these fears I found upon your own demeanour.
>
> Dickens, *Nicholas Nickleby* (1839)

> Never yield to force; never yield to the apparently overwhelming might of the enemy.
>
> Churchill, speech at the Harrow School (1941)

As in the previous section, most of the examples so far have involved isocolon – that is, parallel structure. But this pattern, too, can also be used to polish a reversal of structure, or chiasmus. Whereas a strong ending makes a chiasmus sound decisive, the unstressed finish ends it with a something closer to a flourish.

> Woe unto them that call evil good, and good evil; that put darkness for light, and light for darkness; that put bitter for sweet, and sweet for bitter!
>
> Isa. 5:20

> "Oh! sir," answered Jones, "it is as possible for a man to know something without having been at school, as it is to have been at school and to know nothing."
>
> Fielding, *Tom Jones* (1749)

> Signs and wonders, eh? Pity if there is nothing wonderful in signs, and significant in wonders!
>
> Melville, *Moby-Dick* (1851)

> It's an epitome of life. The first half of it consists of the capacity to enjoy without the chance; the last half consists of the chance without the capacity.
>
> Twain, letter to Edward Dimmitt (1901)

4. *Sound and sense (cont.).* Moving from a strong to a weak rhythm – that is, from a clause that ends with a stress to a clause that ends without one – works especially well

when the shift follows the substance. This pattern lends itself to claims of a "not this but that" kind. The strong ending of the negative part of the sentence pulls up on the reins. The soft ending of the affirmative part lets them go.

Dickens, *Great Expectations* (1861)	Take nothing on its looks; take everything on evidence.
Macaulay, *The History of England* (1849)	The Puritan hated bearbaiting, not because it gave pain to the bear, but because it gave pleasure to the spectators.
Stephen, *Liberty, Equality, Fraternity* (1873)	The minority gives way not because it is convinced that it is wrong, but because it is convinced that it is a minority.
Bierce, *Ashes of the Beacon* (1905)	He struck at government, not because it was bad, but because it was government.

Perhaps the best use of the movement from strong to weak endings comes when the first part of a sentence makes a strong claim and ends on a stressed syllable. Then the second part uses milder language of concession, conciliation, or weakness, with a soft syllable at the end to reinforce it.

Johnson, in Boswell's *Life* (1791)	Small debts are like small shot; they are rattling on every side, and can scarcely be escaped without a wound: great debts are like cannon; of loud noise, but little danger.
Burke, *Reflections on the Revolution in France* (1790)	By hating vices too much, they come to love men too little.
Carlyle, *The French Revolution* (1837)	With arms we are an unconquerable man-defying National Guard; without arms, a rabble to be whiffed with grapeshot.

Only the silence of the boat was at intervals star-
tlingly pierced by one of his peculiar whispers,
now harsh with command, now soft with entreaty.

Melville, *Moby-Dick* (1851)

Originality consists in thinking for yourself, not
in thinking differently from other people.

Stephen, *Liberty, Equality,
Fraternity* (1873)

Every man is important if he loses his life; and
every man is funny if he loses his hat and has to
run after it.

Chesterton, *Charles Dickens*
(1911)

A NOTE ON THE TYPE

*Farnsworth's Classical English Style has been set in Sabon
Next, a type with a distinguished and complex history. Originally com-
missioned in the 1960s from the master typographer, designer, and callig-
rapher Jan Tschichold, Sabon is a contemporary interpretation of a roman
type attributed to Claude Garamond and an italic attributed to Robert
Granjon. It was named in honor of Jacques Sabon, a punchcutter who
worked for the printer who created the specimen on which Tschichold
based his design. Because the types were initially intended for machine
composition on both Linotype and Monotype as well as for hand composition, the design was carefully drawn and modified to accommodate the
limitations imposed by the various methods of composition. This process
resulted in a widely popular type that was somewhat compromised by its
lack of kerns, a feature that limited the appeal of the italic in particular.
Sabon Next was drawn in 2002 by Jean François Porchez, who set out to
harmonize Tschichold's type and the types that inspired it with the possi-
bilities that the OpenType platform offered to the contemporary type
designer. The result is an elegant, highly readable type with a complete
range of characters (including a generous selection of ligatures, swash
characters, and ornaments) that is beautifully suited to book work.*

DESIGN & COMPOSITION BY CARL W. SCARBROUGH

1970–2020
David R. Godine
⚕ Publisher ⚕
FIFTY YEARS